A JOURNEY TOWARDS HAPPINESS

On A Path Paved With Little Poems

Aufie Zophy @ Hans Van Rostenberghe

INDIA • SINGAPORE • MALAYSIA

ISBN 979-8-89673-368-3

Contents

Poems

Executive Summary

The book starts with a poem about a tiny purple flower, achieving its essential purpose of being appreciated for its beauty and experiencing ultimate happiness. Subsequently the author takes you on a path of poems and short essays with gems of wisdom covering some essential elements of living a life filled with happiness and peace of mind. He takes you on a poetic voyage that will unmistakably awaken your awareness about some of the biggest gifts that life offers us on a daily basis. He 'll enkindle the peace from without and from within. He will put your heart and soul on fire for experiencing beauty with all your senses. The most exquisite poetic diamonds you will find in the chapter on love and kindness. He takes you then on a trip of creativity and courage, before a concluding piece on the significance of our contributions to the world.

Foreword

It was a very sunny day in March 2010. I had planned a 1-day trip to a nearby island with my two sons, who were aged 14 and 15 years. By 9.00 we were at the jetty and a speed boat was about to leave. We counted ourselves lucky to still be allowed as extra passengers on the boat.

The sea was rough and the boat was going fast, jumping on the waves. I sat in the front of the boat and one big wave threw me a bit in the air. When I landed on my buttocks, the boat already was moving up on another big wave, which made it a very hard landing. I felt a sudden extremely sharp pain in my back. The rest of the journey was excruciating and upon getting home much later that day, I could barely walk. My wife brought me to the hospital and every single small pothole in the road was a small torture to my back.

A burst fracture of my first lumbar vertebra had happened. Luckily, the nerves seemed not to be affected and I could move my legs normally and sensation was intact. The verdict of the bone specialist: 3 months of flat rest on bed. I got a jacket, that kept me in the right position.

Even reading a book was not easy while lying down. Instead, I listened to audiobooks. The first audiobook was about leading with soul and it contained a wonderful poem by William Blake, titled 'Eternity'. I found it on the internet, on a website called PoemHunter. Apparently, anyone could register and post own poems on the site. I had written some poems, years ago, but only in my mother tongue, Flemish.

I was sitting outside, or more precisely, lying outside when I saw a group of extremely small purple flowers in the grass. They were lovely, but so small, I had never really paid any attention to them at all. One was particularly beautiful and with some overstretching of my arms I managed to take a beautiful close-up picture of it. In my imagination I felt the feelings of the tiny flower and my first English poem was born. It went straight on the website I mentioned before and within days, I got so many touching comments on it, that I was really motivated to write more "poetry" in English. I use inverted commas since I felt initially that my attempts at poetry were looking more like nursery rhymes than like what poetry was meant to be.

It has been fashionable for far too long for poetry to be like a soup of words, nice words, around a theme, but very hard to understand or even guess what was meant by it all. I have read so many award-winning poems and all too often the message got really lost in the style and even though there was some sensual pleasure in reading the words, there was no clearly understood message, no spiritual pleasure in reading the poetry.

When I read the essay of RW Emerson, titled the poet, I gained some insight that not all poetry had to be a hard-to-understand soup of words. He wrote: "*The sign and credentials of the poet are that he announces that which no man foretold. He is the true and only doctor; he knows and tells; he is the only teller of news, for he was present and privy to the appearance which he describes. He is a beholder of ideas and an utterer of the necessary and causal. For we do not speak now of men of poetical talents, or of industry and skill in metre, but of the* **true poet.**" And Emerson went on: "*For it is not metres, but a metre-making argument that makes a poem, a thought so passionate and alive that like the spirit of a plant or an animal, it has an architecture of its own, and adorns nature with a new thing. The thought and the form are equal in the order of time, but in the order of genesis the thought is prior to the form. The poet has a new thought; he has a whole new experience to unfold; he will tell us how it was with him, and all men will be the richer in his fortune. For the experience of each new age requires a new confession, and the world seems always waiting for its poet.*"

Reading the above message of a giant in both poetry and philosophy, like Emerson opened up my mind. I did no longer long to make poems that seem cryptic, mystic and difficult to understand. It was OK to have a clear meaning, a superb message within each poem, as long it was brought in a beautiful, original and, if possible, melodious way.

Throughout my life I have been thinking a lot about happiness, about my life's purpose and my profession as a university-based neonatologist (specialist for premature and sick new-borns). This has really helped me grow into a deeper understanding of the matter. I am convinced that the road to happiness is a happy road. All side streets leading towards that road are made up of some unmovable principles of virtues. The road is adorned with peace, beauty, love and creativity. I am sure that the reader of this book will gain so much enthusiasm to reach that road, enjoy every step on it and inch every day a bit closer towards our aim of ultimate happiness.

The road to happiness is paved with little poems. The book contains small simple poems, and mostly light wisdom; sometimes a bit more complex poems and a bit of heavier wisdom. It is meant to be enjoyed in small sips, in bite-sized reading. I do not encourage anyone to read the whole book at once. Ideal bite-size is perhaps three poems or short essays per day. Some bites will make you smile, at some times you will revel in delight, at other times, you may frown a little. It is all part of that fantastic road.

I think you will get most out of the book by reading it from front to the end, because there is a logical sequence inside, but if you feel like diving in, right in the middle of the book, feel free to enjoy any part of it at any time.

I want to start with some little verses, a poem, titled, 'Arete'. Arete is an old Greek term for excellence, a kind of perfection based on virtue. It was also the name a Greek Goddess that stood for this. Another meaning of the word, arete, is the sharp edge of a mountain. Please sit back, relax and enjoy:

Arete

I picture a world,
Where in every family,
Each member, every day
Brings an uplifting poem
To the dinner table

Arete

I picture a world,
Where in every classroom,
Each student, every day
Brings an uplifting poem
To share with each other

Arete

I picture a world,
Where for every friendship event,
Each friend, every time
Brings an uplifting poem
To share with all

Arete

Now let us start the journey on that amazing road!

HAPPINESS

Little Purple Flower

I am a little purple flower
My petals so extremely small
I 've stood in the grass for many an hour
Enjoying a breeze most of all

But, oh, what happened to my peers!
Just yesterday, it moved me to tears
While the children of John were playing their game
My peers were trampled to death, what a shame

When just before that, some bigger flowers were damaged
The children were scolded badly by John
But when my brothers were ravaged
It was noticed, sadly, by none

Today, however, I had a reason to smile
A nerd, or so he must be
Looked at this little purplish flower, a while
And took a picture of me

Even if tomorrow, to the worst of my fears
I have to die, as yesterday my peers
I will do so happily
since someone has seen the beauty in me.

Peace on you.

I hope you enjoyed the story of the little purple flower. While this poem was open for comments on a public poetry website, one comment read: "I hope this little purple flower never dies". The reader had found true compassion for this little lucky flower.

While many of the other little purple flowers had died, before anyone had noticed their beauty, this one was the lucky one, the happy one. This one had fulfilled its own purpose.

The road to happiness seemed simple and short for this flower, but how about us, humans?

Searching for Happiness

Most of us are in search for happiness

We search for wealth, pleasure, comfort and power and assume that happiness will follow more or less automatically. Once we achieve a decent level of wealth, pleasure and comfort, many feel not too happy still, not too satisfied, and go and search for more wealth, more pleasure and comfort, and more power. This results not rarely in an endless search. It is not rare for multi-millionaires to feel they do not have enough.

Luckily, more and more people are discovering the giant truth that happiness is found more easily in a life of purpose, a life of service. Our little purple flower found her purpose in a life of beauty. Supreme happiness did not imply endless strife for pleasure, wealth or power.

Simple service, and a life of purpose,
and fully embracing all gifts, life gives to us
bring us enough happiness to have a good life,
without us having to pursue an endless search for anything...

Peace of Mind

It brings so much peace to give
to give something of value for free
It brings so much peace to serve
To serve someone purely from the heart
So much peace of mind is found in love
To love someone unconditionally
It brings so much peace of mind to be kind
Kindness is truly the new smart

Aufie Zophy

Purpose

Peace of mind is perhaps one of the most essential ingredients of happiness.

If we have goals that are not bringing us peace of mind, we may reconsider whether these goals are the right goals for us.

Setting a goal and achieving it, does give a boost to our self-perception.

It makes us feel good about ourselves. When we reach the goal, we are happy.

That great feeling, however is often only temporary. I have experienced to fall temporarily into a pit of nothingness, after achieving some major goals:

When I was studying at university level, each year again during that period of end-of-year exams, I longed so much for the final day of the exams. During the exams I felt a certain drive, but the stress of sitting for the exams was big. When finally, the exams were over, and I had obtained the good results I had worked for, I felt a bit lost. Suddenly the holiday was there, and the pleasure of being in drive, working hard towards an noble thing, was gone.

Goals drive us, not rarely bring us in a state of flow and getting nearer to them is a thrill.
But once a goal is achieved, it tends to lose some of its glamour.

Purpose is a bit different.
Purpose is the reason for being here.
Something we are passionate about
A superior aim in our life.
It may be more something we grow into rather than achieve
It is pulling us to itself.

Living a life in which we grow slowly towards that purpose,
is living a life filled with peace of mind, filled with feeling good,
filled with the truest and highest level of happiness.
Goals may change with time, we may adjust our goals;
Purpose is a bit more fixed. It is some bigger ultimate aim,
More principle, a bit less tangible.

Through deep reflection we can discover our purpose
Discovering our purpose is perhaps the biggest thing,
we can do for ourselves and for the rest of the world.
I believe that we were born with a purpose.
Our unique talents and skills as a human, enable us to achieve a certain purpose.
If we are not sure about it, we can easily discover it by thinking about what our passion is, by reflecting in silence or by making some time, some solitary time in the most beautiful part of nature.

When we have discovered our purpose of our life,
We can set our goals more effectively.
We may adjust our goals along the way,
But our purpose tends to stay until the end.

I hope you enjoy the next poem:

Written in the Sand

It is written in the sand
The purpose of our life
Millions of grains of sand

If the sea 'd have erased it from the shore
The grains will have whispered it to the drops
And waves, the braking waves will sing
The purpose of our life

If the heat of day erased it from the surf
Evaporating mist 'll carry it to the clouds
Where they will paint it in amazing skies
The purpose of our life

The clouds will rain and
And diamond beads will ornament the rose
The rose's scent will tell it
The purpose of our life

But if we fail to find it
In the sand or song of waves
In the clouds or scent of roses
The purpose of our life

We may have to make it quiet
And look deep within our heart
Where it will be dancing all around
The purpose of our life.

If we do not find it in our hearts,
We may have to return to sand
It is written in the sand.

Aufie Zophy

The Power of Reflection

I just thought about the world.
I just thought about myself.
I really feel this type of reflection is a true essential element of mental well-being.

Without regular reflection, we tend to just live on.
If we do not reflect on where we are, and where we are going,
we tend to be swiped up and down by the waves on the ocean
a bit like a plastic bottle is going up and down on the waves.

With regular reflection, really thinking about our day, and keeping our purpose of life in front of our eyes, we tend to be able to swim steadily through the waves like dolphins.

The waves, up and down will be definitely there in each of our lives,

but choosing to reflect on our life, on the world, on our own behaviour,
will determine the effect of the wavy ocean that makes up the circumstances of our life.

We can "swim" steadily in the direction of our purpose, and of our short-term goals.

Please make some time for reflection. Maybe the most valuable thing we can do,

for ourselves, for others and yes... for the world.

6 Little Bits

Looking up at the sky, a bit of happiness, a smile
Seeing a wonderful tree, a bit of happiness, an idea
Hearing the song of a bird, a bit of happiness, a melody
Feeling the crisp morning breeze, a bit of happiness, a good feeling
Sipping a cup of hot coffee, a bit of happiness, a great taste
A moment of reflection, a bit of happiness, a grateful heart

Just 6 moments and all these bits
added up to quite a lot... :) 😀

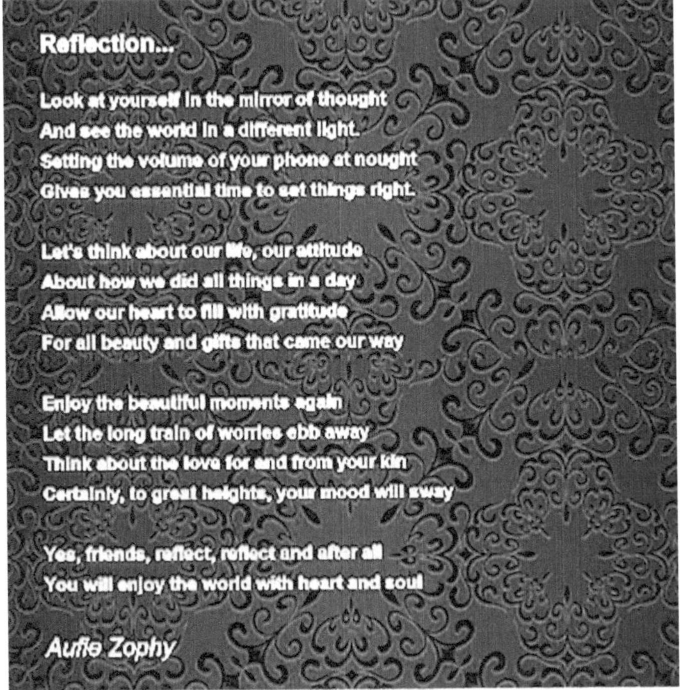

Here is a wonderful quote from RW Sockman:

*"Our growth depends not on
how many experiences we devour,
but on how many we digest."*

Success or Happiness?

Whatever our aim in our life,
Whether it is to be rich as Buffet
Beautiful as Angelina or Pitt
Whether it is professional success
going to that perfect vacation
or setting up that fantastic charity

we always expect that reaching the aim will bring us
happiness
Is there any true success without happiness?

Some time ago, I read a book, titled, 'awakening brilliance and the teachers using the methods explained in the book, were using some sessions during school time to ask the pupils, what was making them really happy.

What a great idea to encourage students to reflect and find the foundation of their life's purpose. The book made me think about myself and what had made me happy so far. Enjoy the poem below

Happiness

I guess it was my auntie's fault
That before I was six years old
It were my looks that made me happy
She just never stopped praising me

Later when I went to school
I realised I was a bit of a fool
To be so proud about my looks
My happiness shifted towards my books

Oh yes, I studied so hard
Most kids and my teachers thought I was smart
Every time I came home with good grades
Wow, that is fantastic! I was praised

But then came the teenage years
Happiness depended on approval of peers
My marks did not earn me any admiration
My looks had undergone some deterioration

I had grown fat and puberty came late
I got pimples, making it all still less great
I had grown into quite an unpopular kid
Happiness? I seemed to grow far away from it

Throughout my youth however
There was a place, I was let down never
It was my home, it was the presence of mother
She cared for her kids, truly like no other

After puberty, my appearance improved a bit
Even though I am still not too proud of it
My grades allowed me to further my education
But happiness is another equation

I realise now that being fully happy
Is lying not so much outside of me
My biggest asset is still the care I received
Even though my mother has already deceased

She equipped me with a caring personality
and that is exactly what makes me happy
I get peace of mind while caring for another
Thanks to the great example of my loving mother

I have also appreciated my spiritual life
Imparted by mother and also my wife
When to our source, we try to connect
Life comes so close to being perfect

Another source of happiness has been
The magical beauty of nature, I 've seen
I love to spend time on the beach to unwind
That's where wisdom seems to pour in my mind

If I am allowed to summarise,
Since long I came to realise
That happiness is truly lying within after all
In wisdom, in love, in a beautiful soul.

Journey

I think it is quite a cliche to call life a journey but I think the saying is so successful because there is so much value in it.

Our big destinations are often not as great as we imagined all along the way and soon after reaching a destination, we need to start the next journey. If I can give the example of medical students, once they finish their studies, as medical student, then only begins housemanship with so much of night work. Then the specialisation, the subspecialisation, then establishing of themselves... Life seems like a never ending journey with ever changing destinations.
So if we want a happy life, we cannot postpone the happiness until we finally reach, because we may die before we reach the ultimate destination. We have to make the journey enjoyable. Studying can be enjoyable. If we just develop enough curiosity, if we just get enough excited about gaining new knowledge it does not have drudgery at all. And so is it with each next leg of our lifelong journey. It is possible to develop the right mind set to make it truly enjoyable.
Keeping our purpose at the front of our mind, we will see opportunities, we will remain focused on the good

A Matter of Focus

Many times, our life is a bit like the picture above.
The bottom part is filled with not so nice things,
but the top is amazingly beautiful, isn't it?

Some people tend to focus about half of the time on each
Some people tend to focus 90% of the time on the dirt
Some people tend to focus 90% of the time on the beauty

While it would be madness to completely ignore the dirt
We can accept that our life is not perfect
and go on and enjoy all beautiful things in it

Let us be wise enough to deal with the dirt
clean it where we can, accept it will never be perfectly clean
and then enjoy all beauty :) (for at least 90% of the time)

What a Power!

At any time we see only a very small part of the whole world.
We see only our own garden, or the book in front of us,
maybe more often, we see only the screen in front of us,
or the person that does something we like,
or the person that does something we don't like.

That is such an extremely small, minuscule part of the world.
And even a much smaller fraction of the universe.

The nice thing about the above thoughts,
is that actually we **can** choose what to look at, at any time.
We can even choose how to look at it (with an open mind,
with an angry heart, from a distance, as a bystander
as a victim,....).

If we become aware of this **power** to choose,
our whole life may become a bit different.
We do not need to be just undergoing what is happening,
we can choose to observe it or not,
to be involved in it or not,
to like it or not.

If we do not like it, we can choose to focus on something else.
It sounds, easy. It is initially not easy.
It requires some exercise.
Our mind is actually under our control
We say: my mind, meaning the mind of me

That me, that I who owns the mind
is not the mind. It is the higher self.
If our mind refuses to let go of a negative thought,
we can choose to think about something else and
the mind has to release anyhow.

Focus on Aim

(inspired by R. Sharma's the monk who sold his ferrari)
I like the part of Alice in Wonderland where Alice asks the rabbit which way she should go. The rabbit responded that it depended on where she wanted to go. When Alice said she did not know where to go, the rabbit responded that then it did not matter which way she would take.

If we have no aim in our life, we may just drive around in circles and 10 years from now, we may be at exactly the same level of achievement that we are now.

So important to take on and off some time and think about our aim in the short term, medium long term and long term. Best to write it down. Why to write it down?

1. It will allow us to get focused: Think about a few rays of sunlight. If not focused, they give a little bit of warmth. If focused through a magnifying glass: can light up a flame.
    Focus can convert our aim in to small flame that may give us light and warmth.
2. If we write down and read our aim, it will tell our subconscious mind that this thought is more important than the other 59 999 thoughts we think in a day.

A wonderful quote of Jawaharlal Nehru:

**Failure comes only
when we forget our ideals
and objectives and principles**

Goals

While driving my car,
I listened to a man talking about goal setting.
And I think he had something interesting to say.

It was about wanting **to be** the person we dream of
rather than wanting **to get** that thing we dream of
or wanting **to do** that action we dream of.

He said too often our goals are to get that car,
to get that house to get that amount of money,
or to make that trip around the world
to do this or that extreme sport

Before we *can get and do* extraordinary things
we have *to be* extraordinary people,
and to be truly extraordinary
means invariably to be kind
means invariably to be loving
to be humble, honest and good.

Along the way, however, not rarely, worry creeps in, anxiety,
nervous tension,..
At these moments falling back on our purpose and aims, and
getting back things in focus is super important.

Life is Not Easy But Beautiful

Anxiety, nervous tension
Adrenaline running in veins
Stress seems the only dimension
Impossible to keep it in reins

Some storms indeed come our way
Peak winds we have to endure
Hurricanes however, not long do they stay
How to recover, where is the cure

As the strength of the wind slows
We can change the focus of mind
Pretty flowers can get us out of the lows
A forest, a sunset, a friend who is kind

Life is most of the time not easy
But if we do look for beauty
Stress will most likely ease
Mind may come to peace

Ten and One Hundred

Today, I received ten challenges from our God.
Some were easy, some were hard.
Some were hurting some were not.
Some were mere imperfections in my heart

Our Creator sent also a hundred gifts my way
Some were truly great and miraculous
Some seemed common and mine every day
Each made my soul feel a bit more fabulous

Today, I managed to deal with the challenges
And then make time to focus on the gifts
I regret the days, I was focused only the ten challenges
And became not even aware of the one hundred gifts.

Gifts

Living a life with a purpose, journeying along this not so easy but beautiful path, we can enjoy happiness. There is one thing that makes happiness and pure peace of mind a bit easier to achieve: **awareness.** We can allow ourselves to be aware, or to be more aware of the wonderful gifts that the universe, our Creator of the universe is giving to us on a daily basis.

Big, Big Presents

Isn't it always fun and pleasant
To receive a wonderful present?
Wrapped in paper and ribbons of gold
A gift of value and beauty untold.

Unexpected or on a special event!
Received from a brother or friend;
Surely happy feelings will be there.
But what if the gift is floating in air?

Every day we get such gifts for free.
Think just about all the beauty we see;
The peace we find at dawn in our room;
The song of a bird, a marvellous tune.

There is so much in nature to be adored
Which gets all too often simply ignored
So is also the love that sits in our heart
And the creativity, our sense for art.

The love sits in our heart; be always aware:
It is replenished no matter how much we share
Sharing love, the greatest gift we get from God
But all too often we appreciate it not.

Creativity another gift from above
As valuable for our character as love.
Using our talents as well as we can
for helping any other woman or man

Most of the gifts of nature are always there
We just need to open our heart and let it in
Love and creativity in abundance to share
So let's all be aware and live a life from within

Aufie Zophy

Awareness of Pleasure, Happiness Beyond...

The Pleasure of Food

Pleasure lies in consuming food when we are hungry. Wonderful!

Having a superb dinner in a nice and cozy restaurant. Wonderful!

Certainly, a family dinner, super pleasurable!

Some of us get so enthralled by this pleasure, that we keep eating.
We accumulate fat, get overweight, obese and make ourselves feel not comfortable. We may even get sick and die early. The pleasure that lies in food is not unique to humans:
the fly in the sky, the fish in the sea, the birds in the trees, the chicken, the cow; all of them find pleasure in eating.

Other Pleasures That Help Sustain Life

There are other pleasures that are related to sustaining life too. They are wonderful too. It is good to enjoy them at appropriate times, but if we make them a purpose by itself or get too excited about such pleasures, we may overindulge, which invariably makes us feel not comfortable and they may make us sick and even cause us to die prematurely.

Awareness

We are human. And as humans, we were gifted with pleasures and sources of happiness beyond those that are needed to sustain life. The key to experiencing the pleasures and happiness beyond those we share with the animal kingdom lies in AWARENESS.

Beauty

One such pleasure is beauty. We need to be *aware* of the beauty that is all around us, in order to experience fully its pleasure

My garden has thousands of flowers. Tens of them, I planted but hundreds, literally hundreds have grown spontaneously, in the wild. The very small flowers, half-hidden in the grass, the flowers on the clover, on the weeds, on the trees, on the shrubs, each of them displaying their own little bit of exquisite beauty.

And yet there are days, when I dash from my door to my gate, without paying any attention, without any awareness that there is so much beauty along my way for all of us to see.

Every morning, a chorus birds sings beautiful songs, but all too often we are too much in a rush, too busy with our small tasks, to stop and listen, to really become AWARE of it and enjoy the pleasure that lies in listening to these beautiful sounds.

Just this morning, I made a small walk on the beach and the sky was so amazing. Sun rays radiated over very dark background clouds and made the sea below them, white. It looked like a painting where they display an apparition of God.

Surely the beauty of nature, the beauty for our eyes, the beauty for our ears are a source of pleasure and happiness. Somehow, we have to make time for it, look for it, look at it, listen for it, listen to it, in order to consciously enjoy the true beauty. We need to be aware! We can consciously make time for beauty and increase our level of happiness instantly by enjoying the beauty all around us.

Beauty is only one of the pleasures beyond animal experience. Another one is...

Peace

If we consciously experience the peace that we have, the peace at night, just before we go to sleep or the fabulous peace in the morning, just after waking up, ... During these minutes or even hours just before or after sleep, do we consciously enjoy the peace that is within them? Right now, even, it is quiet in my room and the rain and winds of the monsoon season are the only sounds I hear. I try to relax my body, to quiet my mind and to focus on the silence, on the rain. I close my eyes and experience peace, which is a joy to our soul, a pleasure to our body and bliss for our hearts.

Sometimes we pray for peace and expect it to come from someplace far away, to descend on us from heaven or from the skies. But peace is most of the time all around us. All we need to do is make it a bit silent within become aware and consciously experience and enjoy the peace.

Love

And then there is love, a truly big one, perhaps the most misunderstood source of happiness. When I pray for love, I get sometimes the same feeling as when praying for peace. We expect it to come from outside, from somewhere far away, but if we truly look inside of our own heart, there are tons of love sitting right there.

There are two kinds of love: the love we get (like friendship) and the love we give (like friendliness). We crave for true friendship, we crave to get love and appreciation, but it is not in our hands, not under our control. That is indeed depending on others, whether or not we get love and friendship.

But the other love, the love we can give, the friendliness, is really within our control. When we were born, our heart was filled with love, and we started to smile at our parents and give away our loving feelings. And what did we get back? Currents, torrential currents of mother's love and father's love. Actually, all the love and friendliness that was planted in our hearts at birth, is still in our hearts. It sits there and the more we give it away, the faster it gets replenished. It is as if there is a source, an ocean, filling our heart with love, as soon as we give a bit away. There is so much friendliness in our hearts. We give it away and poof, it is replenished by new and fresh friendliness.

If we become AWARE of this huge reserve, this giant heap of love that sits in our heart and soul, and we start to give it away consciously, it is such a big source of peace of mind and happiness. Maybe the biggest source of happiness and joy that we can ever experience. Somehow, we were programmed by our Creator or by the universe to enjoy this very special human source of true happiness. It gives us the greatest possible level of satisfaction and feeling good whenever we truly give away the love that sits in our heart, whenever we manage to genuinely help some of those around us, whenever we manage to make a positive difference and create a smile on the face of a human being. Love is here, it is here now, and it is always easy to find, as long as we look for it where it sits: inside.

While beauty and peace are joys, we can experience passively, since they are like real presents, like birthday gifts, given to us by the universe or God, love is special in a way that it was planted in our heart and only if we give it away, we will experience the great human joy connected to it. And the love we tend to pray for most, the one we get, the friendship will flow like a natural consequence to us in great quantities. And even if it doesn't, the joy of sharing the love in our hearts with others is always worth it by itself. I have personally experienced multiple times the great paradox: "it is in giving that we receive".

Creativity, Growth, Devotion, Self-expression

Beauty and peace, we can enjoy passively. Giving love and creativity require more action. There is joy in creating a work of beauty and actively maintaining or even creating peaceful situations for our loved ones. There is joy in growth: personal growth, emotional growth, spiritual growth that we tend to obtain through sincere (prayerful) reflection about the challenges in our lives. Through reflection comes wisdom and there is a great pleasure in making positive difference through the sharing of wisdom that we gained over years of experience. Self-expression and living a life of purpose are among the greatest sources of joy and happiness.

The Story of Mr. Robot!

Imagine you create a robot.
It is so important that the battery gets charged on and off.
So you program Mr. robot to feel low if the battery is low
and to experience some pleasure when the battery is charged.

The purpose of Mr. robot is that he helps people
and that he is always friendly and good.
So you program the robot to feel very good when he does that.
He feels great satisfaction and a superb peace and happiness
if he helps, is friendly and good.

Then you start up the robot and you have big expectations.
The robot is starting his 'life' and to your big frustration,
he is spending almost all of his time 'running' after the small pleasures
you had installed when he did the things necessary for maintenance.
He completely ignores his main purpose and
remains most of the time ignorant of the huge benefits for him
you had installed when he would be helping people.

Stupid Robot!

A Bit of Bliss

Swallowing every day a bit of bliss, I try
Soft amazing light in the pastel morning sky
The song of a bird, singing passionately
The outline of a gently swaying tree

But if I wake late, all this beauty I may miss.
Then, at work, I still try to find some bliss
In the superb opportunities for caring
In all the love and kindness we are sharing

Still if at work, I was only busy and stressed,
The evening may be super blessed
The love of family, a toddler's kiss
Truly, every day, I try to get a bit of bliss.

For every day, every hour, I wish too
a truckload filled with bliss for you.

Based on the above, the next chapters will focus on some of the most precious gifts of life:

Peace, one of the most fantastic gifts: peace of the early night or the morning: all we have to do is think about it, let it in and be fully aware of it and enjoy it. We may have to clear our busy mind a bit of all the clutter that worried or angered us earlier in the day, but peace is a great gift, not difficult to experience

Beauty is another one of these supreme gifts from the universe. It may require a bit more action than peace: we have to actively look for it or listen for it. Still, with a minor effort, we will enjoy it, and our life becomes a bit more beautiful. Just take the time to look up at the skies, the trees, the flowers.

Love. It sits in our heart but to fully enjoy it, we have to let it flow. The gift of love keeps flowing: the more we give away, the more flows back in. Giving love, even if no love comes back to us, is pure joy. But it is almost impossible to give away love without receiving any back. To turn a smile on someone's face...

And the fourth one is **creativity**. For this, we have to listen to our heart and our deepest passion let it boil over and express in a nice and original way. Perhaps a bit more difficult than enjoying peace, beauty or love, but it is surely worth it, to make some extra efforts. RW Emerson wrote: a man is only half himself and the other half is his expression. I agree quite a bit with that. We truly need to express ourselves and if we manage to inspire even only one other person, it is a true source of joy.

Intermezzo

Before we embark on the PATH of joy, reading poetry about peace, beauty, love and creativity, I have a brief intermezzo. It starts with a poem, titled the girl with a broken heart:

The Girl with a Broken Heart

A heart filled with pain, deceived by lies.
Feelings, bitter and hard; hatred burning.
A flood of tears, giving her all red eyes.
Will the tide ever be turning?

Even though her heart, he has been destroying,
life seems so nice to him, he is still enjoying.
She is alone, all alone with a heart full of hurt.
She shouts it out loud, but remains unheard.

Lust for revenge, she finds in her heart;
making suffering and pain to be worse.
She wants peace, but where does she start;
all she feels, is hatred. It feels like a curse.

Then she prays for help and support from above,
for her lonely heart that seems to have lost all love.
Soon, the idea of forgiving seems to grow stronger.
She does not want to hate for much longer

Once she manages to forgive in her heart,
grief seems suddenly to start falling apart.
Tears may come back on and off,
but she becomes able to live, love and laugh

Truly the cure for a broken heart
begins when the forgiveness will start.
Whoever decides to keep hatred so strong
will continue to hurt and be bitter all along.

Hatred is like venom that prohibits one to live;
the antidote is to find it in our heart to forgive

NO Grudges

As long as we have not gotten rid of all hatred and grudges in our heart, happiness and true peace of mind may elude us.

It is not easy to forgive, since it appears to us, that in the act of forgiving we set the persons who wronged us so much, free. The truth is that these persons are free, whether or not we have forgiven them.

The only person imprisoned in a cage of negativity, is us, as long we keep grudges and hatred in our heart. Simple but true forgiveness does set us free.

Forgiving an enemy does not mean we start to love them again. It involves a deep inner process of trying to understand why a person with such great limitations did what hurt us so much. It involves pity, empathy and compassion. We may feel that the particular enemy is nor worthy of these principles, but forgiving is not something we do for them, it is something we do for us. We do not want to meet our enemies again, but if we meet them accidentally, we will be free of feelings of hatred. We will try not to meet them again; we remember what they did, but in our heart, there is pity and compassion and no grudges and no hatred.

A heart filled with grudges will not know true happiness.

Forgiveness and gratitude are pillars of a happiness.
Forgiveness is something we can daily for small and big injustices
we encountered
Gratitude requires awareness. Now, we are ready to read our
next chapters, filled with peace, beauty, love, and creativity

PEACE

Silence

Contemplation, searching for my soul
Silence encompassing all
Alone but not in solitude
Silence giving fortitude

My ego-thoughts trying to prop up
Silence makes them stop
Soul is what I'm searching for
Silence, silence I adore

Connecting to my soul
Silence winning after all
Thoughts connect with high above
Silence fills my soul with love

Conscience conquering my mind
Silence makes it look so kind
Soul and conscience hand in hand
Silent wish to never end

Grateful heart joins in
Silence makes it all akin
Thanking God for this silent contemplation
Thanks for silence, thanks again

Aufie Zophy

Yes, of Course,...

Did you have a peaceful day, today?
Did you have a peaceful day, yesterday?
Many times, for many of us, the answer may be "no" to the
above questions.

The next question is: why our life tends not to be peaceful?
And then we come up with a thousand reasons.

All reasons tend to lie outside of ourselves: a mass shooting
in a school,
the world economy, the cuts in the budget, the stress at work,
the nasty traffic, the crossness of my spouse or children,
the friends who are not real friends, and so on, etc. etc.

And yet Peace, the Peace with capital P,
is just present in the air around us.
If we manage to make our minds calm and serene,
we can almost always allow peace to enter our minds.

As humans we were somehow endowed with a fantastic gift:
we are capable of rising above the flight or fight response to
our external circumstances.
Enslaved to our instincts, most of the time we do not make
full use of this fantastic gift.
If the world around seems to go against us, we can take a few
seconds or a minute,

to assess the situation with a positive mindset and avoid to let
the stress hormones
to rush freely through our veins.

Peace is all around is all the time.
Just look at the sky: whether it is pristine blue or covered in
a mass of grey clouds,
the peace in the sky is there. Look at a tree, a flower, a stretch
of grass. Even if you are in a room where you can see none
of these, think about the love, the friendship, the wonderful
message on your social media, the joke that made you laugh
out loud. Peace is really never far away. Even if you can still
not find any of the above, we can always make our mind
quiet, look deep inside of our heart, our soul.

All we have to do, is open our mind, open our mind for peace
and let it in.
Let it flow into our mind from the beauty of our heart and
soul! Let it flow in from the beauty outside!

"Not letting peace flow into our mind,
is like a fish swimming in the water, but refusing to drink.
Soon if a fish does not drink, his body will hopelessly shrink."

And that is exactly what happens to peace:
if we refuse to drink the peace that is around us all the time
If we refuse to open our mind and let peace in
our happiness will shrink under the pressure of stress.

We have to be "busy" with peace
We have to be motivated to make our life peaceful

Many religions have a wish of peace
But power sick religious leaders often give the extremely
stupid direction
to use the wish of peace only to the people of the same
religion.
This is clear nonsense. Give a wish of peace to everyone you
meet.
Do not just do it as a routine but do it mindfully:
if we utter the wish of peace, really try to think about its
meaning, try to feel the peace flowing. Try to imagine for a
while you sending a few electrons of peace a few photons of
peace from your mind to your friend's mind. How wonderful
the world will become!

Let us today be busy with peace.
Open our mind to the peace from the world
Open our mind to the peace from within
Drink it, as a fish is drinking water
do not allow our minds to shrink
under the pressure of stress.

Love, look for beauty, be grateful for what we have
and experience the peace
If tomorrow someone asks: did you have a peaceful day.
The answer will be "yes of course"

Q..... World Peace

How many of us do sincerely pray for world peace
How many just think it is an illusion
If we go on not praying for world peace
If we go on thinking it is an illusion
Just an illusion it may remain.

Aufie Zophy

A Wave of Peace

Peace

I dream of
a wave of peace

A giant wave of peace
Reaching beyond the fences
Moving deep inside

A wonderful wave, white and blue
Drenching all the minds of my friends
Penetrating deep in each of their hearts
Changing our souls forever

A tsunami of tender loving peace
Devastating all giant walls that consist of greed
Destructive to violent thoughts and feelings
Ripping apart perversion. Erasing arrogance
That superior wave of peace reigning solidly

A wave of peace, streaming
enveloping the world in full
Softening hearts of friends and foes
Wisening our leaders forever

Just peace
Dare to dream with me
Let us all pray together

Let's believe in and awesome
wave of peace

Peace

Aufie Zophy

Let There Be Peace

Our dear God
Let there be peace in my heart
and my soul will be on a path
in the most beautiful forest

Let there be peace in my family
and our hearts will enjoy harmony
and endless bliss

Let there be peace in my village
and our minds will enjoy love
and kindness will reign

Let there be peace in my country
and happiness will be the norm
devout of all stress and frustration

Let there be peace in the world
and we will be able to tackle problems like never before
and all may enjoy the richness and blessings of mother earth

Peace

Sharing Peace

You know what I did today in my car? Usually I listen to some music or to an uplifting audiobook, but today I decided to do something different:

I imagined that in my car there was an ocean of peace and on every oncoming car or motorcycle I poured a bucket of peace. It was fun. I poured the peace and said out loud: here is a bucket of peace for you. In my imagination the peace flowed all over the front windows into the cars. While standing in front of a traffic light, I pulled a bucket out of the ocean of harmony too and poured it over a few drivers who had already received my buckets of peace. I kept pouring buckets of peace and harmony until I reached my workplace. When I reached, I felt so filled with peace and harmony, more than ever before. It had one of the most pleasant rides to my work and I felt good about it. :)

During my evening reflection I wrote a small poem about it:

Sharing peace
Our heart is only the size of a fist
But it contains an ocean of love
Inexhaustible, wavy, exquisite
Fed by the universe, flowing in from above

Take a bucket with you wherever you go
The ocean will never dry up, let it flow
Pour a few buckets of love over anyone you meet
All are longing for love; a sea of it, they need.

Pouring out that ocean from within to all
Will bring a mountain of pleasure and ease
You and humanity will get filled with soul
Let's fill the whole world with love and peace

A Field of Lavender

A huge field of lavender. I replace one flower by a bubble filled with silence and peace. And then I do the same thing to another flower, and then another. We end up in a field of peace.

I wake up from that beautiful dream and find myself in this amazing place. We don't have to search for peace, we do not have to pray for it, we are right in the middle of it. I become grateful and the colours of that field change to soft pastel of extreme beauty.

A train of thoughts flashes by. The negativity within the thoughts is like a tornado, like a set of needles, breaking all the colourful bubbles of peace. I end up in a barren field of broken lavender flowers of poked peace bubbles and go on and live a hectic day.

But we can stop the crazy tornadoes of negativity. We do not have to listen to all negativity in the news. We do not have to allow us to be swept away by negative emotions. We are in control. We can block the tornadoes, throw away the needles: we can choose simple positive thoughts, live a life filled with love and enjoy the huge field of peace throughout the day, wishing wholeheartedly peace to whomever we meet. Wishing peace to each other is one of the most wonderful things, but to do so sincerely, we need to have peace in our heart.

Bubble of Peace

If you manage to be grateful for a moment or two
A giant bubble of peace starts to envelop you
But then more often than ever should be
For small imperfections or a bit of ennui
We smash that peace, turn it into nought
With a bout of irritation, with a negative thought

The Silence of the Grass

The grass, I sat on, was enveloped in silence;
I sat there in awe and complete reverence.
The twinkly grassy green was pleasing my mind,
When it whispered something really kind:

"No matter how often we got cut, we keep on growing.
Our green blades are forever smiling and brightly glowing.
We catch in our loving arms, leaves falling from trees so high.
We act as soft and gentle carpet to anyone who is walking by:
We cover the soil and protect you from dirtying your feet.
Our loving Creator provides at every moment whatever we need
He has put in our little hearts a pack of tremendous love
And we let it flow, this amazing gift from above.
Please, spread a message of love and peace to all on earth,
Since it is a gift, a message of most incredible worth."

My mind was dazzled, still by the grass' fabulous green
I was still amazed by what I had heard and seen
Now here, I take the message of the grass to share:
Let us all cherish love and peace and take forever care...

Aufie Zophy

Peace

Peace starts
Deep inside,
in our hearts

Peace: gently it blows
Through the magic of silence
It flows, it flows, it flows

Let us find peace where it is
And send it to this great big world
As a little bit of peaceful bliss

Aufie Zophy

Going Into The Night

I need to be alone for a while,
to listen to my soul for a while.

A tear knocks on the door of my heart;
I let it in; a story so sad and hard.

I search for truth and long to be strong.
Truth and strength let me wait for long.

I do not want to go into the night like this;
I pray for guidance, I pray for bliss.

The prayer helps the tear to clean a bit inside:
acceptance, love and hope help me see some light.

The tear leaves through my eye, rolls over my cheek,
it falls on the ground, is left there; I go to sleep.

Aufie Zophy

Spreading Peace

Today, let peace reign in our own house
Accepting imperfections of our spouse
unconditional love for daughter and son
Then let the peace be spread to everyone

18.10.23

Aufie Zophy

Y..... It Must Be Sung

Close your eyes, imagine
All the water of the seas,
Inundating your heart
A deluge of love and peace

Keep them closed, your eyes
And try to feel it deep inside
That silent storm of peace and love
An endless stream never to subside

Then open your eyes, open wide
And try to realise, it isn't just a dream
The fountain's abundant flurry
Soaking your soul with love for real

Feel the hard blowing gusts of wind
Blowing love and peace in soul and mind
Let your heart open up and sing
The song of love and being kind

Do not doubt, do not listen to TV
Love and peace is everywhere around
It must be sung it can't be kept
Just let it flow and ever more abound

Aufie Zophy

Within!

Tonight I was peeping silently in my heart.
You know what I found?
I found peace sitting there
I found an awful lot of kindness planted there
I find so much love, ready to be given away.

Then I was confronting my mind:
Hey, mind, if there is so much peace, kindness and love in my heart,
why do you not make full use of it and let me enjoy it all, every day?

I got to understand that it was not my mind that was to blame.
Mind was just obeying my own choices I made day by day.
It was thinking the thoughts I was wanting it to think.

But I wanted to choose peace, kindness and love all the time.
I was praying for it and searching for it!
Why did I choose the thoughts that brought so often the opposite?

Reason chipped in with a thought:
Perhaps, you are looking for peace, love and kindness in the
wrong place
You seem to keep looking for it and expect it from the outside all
the time
Now you have seen where it really sits, it is perhaps time to start
looking from within.

Aren't we all wanting peace and love and kindness very much?
Let us look for these happiness bringers from within.
In a spirit of gratefulness and forgiving, we look within
and we will find all these things not only to be ours,
but to be so abundantly ours that we want to give them away
that we want to share them with everyone we meet.
And these people, we share it with, will share so much back.
Give it a thought, search within and live love,
live peace, live a life filled with kindness!

The World and the Tree

The wars of the past few years may give you a bit of a difficult time to get into a mood that allows you to enjoy and accept the story of the tree and world. Please read the story again if at first it seems difficult to see the giant truth in it. 😊

The Story of the World and the Tree

When we plant a tree, we want it to become a big tree.
We get this image in our mind of the place where it was planted,
being adorned with this huge nice wonderful tree with a big wide crown.

If we'd go every day to look at the tree, we will not see it growing.
But if we have not seen the tree for a long time, we will notice easily
that it has grown so much.

Now, where is the world in this story?
Here it is:

The world is getting better,
Every day the world is getting better, every year.
Exactly! Just like the tree is growing every day.

The number of peace loving people,
hungering for peace, fairness and happiness
for ALL in this world, is ever increasing.

If you look after a year or so, you may not see the difference.
If you look back a decade or a few decades, you may start to
notice.
Look back a century, and you get this absolute certainty:
The world is turning into a better place to live in, fast.

Not just for the few wealthy (actually, many of them,
blinded by the fallacy that they have to protect and grow
their wealth
and power at all cost, are losing out on peace of mind, rather
than gaining it!).

For all groups of people, life is getting better.
More and more people get to know their true nature:
the true nature of humans is that caring brings peace of mind,
kindness brings happiness, Love (the one with capital letter L)
is the key to a balanced life filled with fulfilment.

Every day the pool of good and kind people increases.
Just like a tree grows every day.
Once the tree has a big crown,
in spring it seems to explode
in young greenness and flowers,
Once we will reach a critical number of kind people,
the world will become overnight an oasis of love and peace.

Let us get all on this train of unconditional kindness now.
This will be to the world, like what rain and fertilizers mean
to the tree.
Smile!

New Me

An almost perfect silence
embraces my body, heart and soul

A whispering fountain of sparks
illuminates my inner thoughts

Herbs of love are sprinkled
on the plainness of my hungry ego

A perfect silence,
light and love
A new me emerges

Y/. A Whiff Of Conscience

A whiff of conscience
whispers in our heart
listening in absolute silence
hearing it, a work of art

A bright flame of goodness
for our eyes to see
A fire of rightness
warmth on our skin to feel

Soft winds of love, so kind
blowing breeze of soul
illuminating our mind
an ideal, an inspirational call

Nectar of honesty
Roses of integrity
Aromas dancing merrily
Cherry blossoms of charity

A whiff of conscience
Sitting somewhere deep inside
Shining throughout the universe
An inextinguishable light

(Bachok,3 July 2014)

Aufie Zophy

Calm

The silence of the night
Gives slowly way
To the silence of sunrise
From the source of lovely dreams
To the fountain of inspiration

The stillness of dawn,
Gives slowly way
To the stillness of the day
From the spring of awe
To the sea of creative verve

The tranquility of noon
gives slowly way
to the calm of the evening
If we carry our calm all day
Peace and love will be ours
Forever.

Aufie Zophy

BEAUTY

There is so much beauty all around us, not only beauty for us to see, but also beauty for us to hear, to feel and to smell and even to taste. I think that too often we forget to really become aware of all types of beauty around us. I am sure you will enjoy the next poem.

Sense-ational

The smell of the sea was more precious,
more lovely than that of a rose in spring
The sounds of the waves, real music
Mozart, Bach, never heard such a thing.

Turquoise blue and green and white surf
caressing so softly the view of my eyes
The wind on my skin, so sweet and soft
so tender and cooling, extraordinarily nice

I tried to smell, feel, hear and see
All at the same time, simultaneously
But this was really much easier said than done
When I looked and listened, the smell was gone

Focusing on smell and the breeze from the skies
gave me the sudden strong urge to close my eyes
I tried again and again to absorb the senses of the sea
And what was first two, became soon a wonderful three.

After some time, I finally could sense all four
It felt like being one with the sea in my core
I felt and smelled and heard and saw
It really had me standing there in awe

I licked my lips and guess what...
I could taste some of the sea's salt

Aufie Zophy

Unblind

Tonight,
I saw the nightly light
Creating a glorious sight
On a field of grass

Then I suddenly realised
That all day long
I had been blinded

Only now at night
I saw the glorious sight
Of nightly light
On the grass

I had not seen any glory
The whole day long
something must 've blinded me

Blinded by sunlight?
Or blinded by buzz?
By clutter and buzz
Of a busy day

Blinded by the rush
By a bout of anger
By things that matter little
I had missed the glory of the day

I had missed the glory
Of all the trees I'd passed
The glory of the grass
Of sea and skies

I had missed the glory
Of all the friendship
Of all the love and kindness
Of everyone I'd met

Oh, my God,
I must have been blind
Blind to all this glory
Blind to all this grace

Please, my God,
Unblind me
So tomorrow I will see
The world in all its glory

The glory of the skies and sea
Of the grass and trees
Of everyone around me
Please god help me see

Aufie Zophy

Theatre in Bachok

This morning, I went to a theatre show in Bachok
I got comfortably seated on the first and only row
with a glass of freshly squeezed watermelon
naturally sweetened to perfection.

The first actress to come on stage
was a butterfly, performing brilliantly
the most elegant dance just in the air
Her wings were brown and white
and then she landed with her feather light feet
on a green leaf of a flowerless tree.

The second actor came on immediately:
a white butterfly doing a rock and roll
The birds came on stage before it was their turn
but who cares about turns in this theatre?
A choir of invisible doves
made their lovely sounds in the background
for an aria of a proud yellow bird.

When my drink was finished,
I was allowed to go on stage
and have a private chat with many actors
They spoke a strange language
but perhaps they understood my heartfelt praise.

Aufie Zophy

Nature

"Nature enhances her beauty to the eye of the loving man"
(RW Emerson)

The above is a quote from the essay, the poet, by RW Emerson, a famous essayist and philosopher from the late 19th century. He was part of a moving force to abolish slavery. In the many essays he wrote, he was addressing real life issues, more than most of the other philosophers.

I like the above quote very much. How many times we pass through the most wonderful natural spots without truly observing its true beauty because we are so absorbed in our thinking process or in a conversation with someone who walks with us.

If we manage to make it silent within, while we spend some time in nature and find the most wonderful bit of love in our own heart, we will see the surrounding beauty with different eyes. We will notice the details that make the scene or the flower, or even the trunk of a tree truly miraculous. We will experience the joy of seeing, hearing, feeling the beauty in a superbly different way.

Let us connect to the love within, make a walk in a piece of nature and notice how nature is enhancing its own beauty to the eyes of a loving man. Allow the poetry to well up in our heart.

Miracle

Life is a miracle
A wonderful tree thrills my eyes
It is a miracle
A magnificent song enters my ears
It is a miracle
A delicious soup amuses my tongue
It is a miracle
The warm sunlight cuddles my skin
It is a miracle
The smell of sweet lavender reaches my brain
It is a miracle

My feet touch the grass while I walk
It is a miracle
An original thought crosses my mind
It is a miracle
A lovely gesture moves my heart
It is a miracle
A heart felt prayer hugs my soul
It is a miracle
Oh yes, life is a miracle
But only if we are aware
of the miracle

Aufie Zophy

Y/. Purple

I took a walk this morning
On the beach
I could see so many flowers
Growing in the wild

All of them were coloured purple
So beautiful
Perhaps God's favourite colour
Is purple

Looking at the bright white sand
So delightful
God's favourite colour could also
Be white

A bush with small yellow flowers
So exquisite
Perhaps God's favourite colour
Is yellow

The sea so blue, the grass so green
So soothing and lovely
Gods favorite colour might as well be
blue or green.

But then on my way back I see again
all the purple flowers
It must be purple
:)

Aufie Zophy

Y// Orchards

If our cities were orchards;
our flats tree huts,
decorated with cherry blossoms
and perfume of jasmine flowers;
our highways babbling brooks,
surrounded by choirs of birds;
and love the universal language;
bridges would be redundant
'cause we all 'd be connected

Soul to Soul

Aufie Zophy

Monsoon

Even the monsoon season has its own beauty, its own charms and can bring joy.

The long downpours with their almost uniform dark grey skies are definitely less enticing than the bright-blue-skied sunny days. But even sitting still, observing the rain, can bring peace and deep reflection.

The moments within the monsoon season where the sun breaks through the thick deck of grey clouds tend to bring a certain excitement, hilarity:

In the Heart of the Monsoon

In the heart of the monsoon
The sky decided to undress
Blue skin and a yellow soul
Rays of light and warmth caress

Bright white teeth on laughing waves
Trees smiling with wet green eyes
Dark cloud above the sea seeming shy
brightening up a bit or at least it tries

But then the cloud decides
The story ends too soon
And streaming rains return
In the heart of the monsoon

Elegant Violence

After five days of gloom
and dark monsoon,
sparks of colour in the sunrise
betray an enticing pause in the season

Strong winds still stand
and sweep up white chunks of water
that jump out of the sea
in violent bouts of elegance

On the Stairs Near the Sea

On the stairs by the sea, sitting down,
I absorb the strength of violent winds.
The waves' white foam has turned brown.
Skies give away only a slit-like glimpse
of their deep and far-away azure beauty.
My heart is melting in the view of a tree;
I feel intimately connected to the wild sea,
while cloudy heavens seem to embrace me.

Y// Love And Beauty, Grace

The universe has given me a million flowers
Just for me to see and smell and adore
Perhaps there were many more
That is exactly what I am grateful for

I enjoyed a thousands of friendship hours
Lovely, touching my heart and my soul's core
Perhaps there were many more
That is exactly what I am grateful for

Oh my God in this big universe
In love and beauty, we are immersed
All we have to do is open our heart and mind
Beauty, love and friendship for all of humankind

Aufie Zophy

An Almost True Story

A cheeky little cloud
kissed secretly
a tree in my garden

I had seen it

and soon the evening sun
gave it happily
a wonderful orange blush.

<u>Aufie Zophy</u>

Goodness and Beauty

For each simple random kind act
A small flower grows in my soul,
For each beautiful flower observed
A random kind act grows in my heart

For each loving smile I give
A dew drop comes to my dreams
For each beautiful dew drop I see
A smile is adorning my face

For each simple truth I speak
My soul is touched by a breeze
For each lovely breeze I feel
A simple truth is revealed

Aufie Zophy

Y// The Beauty Of Reality

I sat in a blue bus, on its side a white line
We rode through a landscape wonderfully fine
and a man sitting in the seat in front of me
was reading the paper absorbing all negativity
while missing completely the beauty of reality

Aufie Zophy

Beauty

Sometimes we travel far and long to see a beautiful town.
Sometimes we travel extreme distances to see an exhibition
of beautiful paintings
Sometimes we have this intense longing to see a faraway
"wonder of the world"
Our 'bucket list' tends to be full

Far or Near

Far away mountains and a deep blue lake:
So much beauty; our breath they take.
But today I saw a common sight
And it gave me just as much delight.

I saw an every-day cloud above the sea
And even, if at first, it looked common to me
It had so much beauty, so much to adore,
that it moved my heart and soul to the core.

Let's not forget that things we see every day,
may carry as much or much more beauty and grace
compared to the picturesque scenes from far away,
Let us value what we have today in our own place.

Let us take a minute right now and

find something of exquisite beauty, right where we are.

If our eyes do no find it, let us use our other senses.

let us feel the beauty of the breeze

or listen to the beauty of the sound of the rain

or put up a favourite song,

smell or taste something beautiful.

Walk around for a while

just giving our attention

to finding beauty in the air

in the colour of the sky,

in the palms of our hands

in the piece of furniture nearest to you

Beauty

I love Beauty
I am sure you love beauty too.

Let us enjoy the beauty of the world around us,
a little more consciously today,
give it a bit more attention
our heart will be filled with…

A Thousand Beautiful Feelings

A thousand beautiful feelings,
ready to fill our heart.

Giving an eye to the colours of the sky
or just the wooden furniture in our room

An ear for the sound of the breeze in trees
or just the tune of a favourite song

A touch of our feet on the grass
or just an unbelievably soft carpet

A smell of an exquisite bouquet
or just a drop of lavender oil

The taste of the sea salt on your lips
or just a delicious cup of coffee

Take a minute right now for beauty;
it is never far away.

Soon a thousand beautiful feelings
Will be filling our heart

Aufie Zophy

Some people say that beauty lies in the eye of the beholder, but I want to argue that some things are intrinsically so beautiful and amazingly pleasing, that no eye of any beholder could ever deny that beauty is there:

The Eye of the Beholder

I wonder:

Is there an eye

of any beholder

that 'd not find beauty

in the overwhelming elegance

of the wondrous shells

I found today

on the shore

The Song Of The Soul

A soul was enjoying the beauty of the beach.
It whispered in the ear of the mind
It gently moved the heart
The mind was quiet
And it could hear soul's wondrous song
The heart was open
And it felt soul's amazing awe and grace
The body relaxed and took a breath
A deep and healthy breath.

Peace and bliss engulfed the man

Aufie Zophy

The Log

A log of wood had washed ashore
The tree was not alive anymore
But its beauty i could still adore.

Unlike the woody beauty of the tree
The story may be very different for me.
What will be left may be only memory.

Maybe what i write or what i do
Can, after my life will have ended too,
Still be cherished and adored by you.

I hope that people still will find
in some simple acts of being kind,
That in a way, I will 've left behind,
Inspiration for heart and mind.

Aufie Zophy

Let It In

Foam, abundant foam on breaking waves
Everyone has seen it
Not everyone has let the beauty of it in

The wonderful orchestra of birds in the morning
Everyone has heard it
Not everyone has let the beauty of it in

The amazing shapes and forms of clouds in the sky
Everyone has seen them
Not everyone has let the beauty of it in.

You could easily add a thousand beautiful things
we have all seen or heard
But we did not take the time to let the beauty in

Let us let in every thing of beauty we encounter
Let it touch our inner mind
Let it touch our heart and the deepest of our soul.

Aufie Zophy

Merging

Saturday morning, a softly wavy sea
So much of beauty, it simply invited me
Soon I was afloat in nature's trance
My whole body moved on the wavy cadence

I merged in the unfathomable oneness of all
My mind, body and heart became only soul
Connected to the immeasurable width of the sea
Even the colours of the sky above, were part of me.

I closed my eyes and felt immensely free
Only aware of peace, love and beauty.
The miracle of life experienced in the sea,
Forever, a most precious part of my memory.

Aufie Zophy

Azure

Undulating azure beauty
of the South China Sea,
tickling soul and mind
with thoughts of pure and kind

The breaking waves, so white
smile at me, their teeth so bright.
They sound like wishing me well
vibrating, penetrating my every cell.

Splashing pearls trigger my imagination:
how amazing, the purest source of inspiration!
Come, my friends, come to the beach too,
and let the waves of the sea inspire you

Aufie Zophy

The Cloud

A sublime white cloud
Hanging above the sea
Fluffy and streaky
Transparent and bright
White and blue
Fully abstract
A marvellous sight

That cloud,
So nice.
No ancient Greek,
Nor Michelangelo
Nor Van Gogh, Nor Picasso
Has ever made anything
Of such astonishing beauty

Such a sublime piece of art
Sculpted, painted,
By the Ultimate Master
Of all Sculptors, painters

White Lines (Haiku)

amazing white lines
light'ning in the darkest skies
Frightening beauty.

Aufie Zophy

Soothing Beauty

Sometimes,
Everything seems to go wrong
Everything seems so depressing
It can go on for quite long,
Until we stop to count our blessings

I had fractured my shoulder
the pain was sharp
My mood got quite deep, quite down,
But then just outside my garden...

I was sitting there quietly
Looking at the South China Sea
The sun made it look bright
Bright brown in front,
Hues of bright green to blue behind
With spots that were really dark,
The shadows of a few scanty clouds

All this seen through a frame of white sand below,
A blue sky above and in perspective,
fresh green branches of trees at the sides
How could I be sad for much longer
With such images in front of me?

One of the clouds moved in front of the sun
And a slight breeze came along
To give a refreshing cool to my cheeks
And blow away the moist that had formed on my forehead.

While the ever-changing shadows of the clouds
Continued to colour the sea in ever changing patterns
Two small birds started to argue with their lovely voices
And were flying through and fro.

The breeze got a bit stronger
and made the coconut leaves do their typical dance
The music of the waves was enriched
by the sound of the rustling leaves

I removed a few dry casuarinas leaves
that just had fallen on my cahier,
from branches swaying softly in the wind

The amazing beauty of the scene had me dreamy, when...
My beautiful wife brought me two of my favourite doughnuts
With a cup of steaming hot coffee.
The pain of the fracture seemed to have become so small...

Night

Imagine the stars come out only once in a decade. Tonight is the long-anticipated night. You pray there will be no clouds and sure enough, the night starts with one of the clearest skies ever, not a single cloud. You are outside, you have a small telescope, especially bought for the occasion. You see the most beautiful spectacle in the sky. While you do not know a thing about constellations, there is so much amazing beauty high above that you are close to ecstatic. With your small telescope you can see even further and you see a lot more wonderful lights in the distant expanse.

Starry Night

I take my most precious silver spoon
And feed my eyes with the tenderness
Of that dark soup full of little shiny stars
Spoon after spoon, a bowl that's bottomless
Until my hungry soul feels filled, all too soon.

Tree

When I reflect upon my day
and if my schedule had been so tight,
that I did not admire at least one tree,
sometimes I still go out at night
to find a wonderful tree
and enjoy its presence in the moonlight

The Sun Never Sleeps

When the dark of the night
Seems to win its fight with the light
We are merely in the shadow of the globe

When emotional pain
Seems to obtain its gain
We are merely in the shadow of our hearts

Moonlight and Stardust

The full moon, yellow in the early night
Between two trees, a ball so soft and light
I plucked from the darkness some magic rays
Mixed them with stardust and a bit of praise

I gave them away to the first person I met
And guess what this perfect stranger said.
I have for you too, some magic rays
Mixed with stardust and with praise.

We felt both peace, filled with soft delight
And let the effects of this very special light
Go on, making us to want forever share
Random kind acts and lots of loving care

If the Moon Could Dream

If the moon could dream,
it would dream
that you and me
filled would be

with unconditional love

It has been all along
in the moon its song
of fine white light,
the song of the night

Love Remained

Endlessly tender, the soft moonlight
is shining on the deserted sandy beach,
calming my workaholic restless mind.
Deep in my soul it seems to reach.

Tiny seashells whiter still than the sand
reflect the moon and seem to be on fire.
the beach becomes a nightly heavenly land,
with sparkles, that move my heart and inspire.

Fluffy clouds in the dark expanse
are writing the name of our God
drawing humbly in the sky, immense:
We love you Lord, thanks a lot,

The gentle waves, a lovely song
whispering peace, peace, peace
it goes on and on, for ever long,
The inside of my heart is now at ease.

Love engulfs the unworldly scene
My skin enjoys the nightly breeze
All the worries of the day,
I cannot find, they melted away.

What remains in the night, is love
pure love...

Aufie Zophy

Dream or Reality?

When the night falls,
my thoughts wander
to the sea of abundance.

My ears listen to Tibetan music.
My eyes dream of lakes and mountains.

My heart visits the land of love.
My soul swims in endless oceans of goodness.

When the night falls,
when silence appears,
when most people sleep,
my thoughts wander...

My eyes see smiles and happy faces.
My ears hear chuckles and laughter.
My soul sees the revolution of kindness.

That huge revolution of kindness getting nearer and nearer
and nearer and nearer and nearer and nearer and nearer.

Soon all of us will see our true nature,
kindness everywhere, greed gone.
My thoughts wander
a bit closer to a dream
but every new day, also
a bit closer to the upcoming real

Are you ready to move into the section on love and kindness?
Before we move, enjoy the next few lines first:

Debate of the Century

Love and peace had a debate
Love, being love, gave the loveliest opening statement
Peace, being peace, fully agreed with Love
Both won the debate and walked out of the room
Each filled with love and peace

Aufie Zophy

LOVE AND KINDNESS

Let the endless river of love
flow **out** of your heart

And the endless river of peace
will flow **into** your mind

The Apple Cloud

In the desert: a scorching heat!
It is the temperature of greed.
In the sky almost uniformly blue,
there is a little cloud too.

Almost magically, it takes the form of a grape.
It swells and grows into a big apple's shape.
And from my wonderful apple cloud,
Sweet drops of wisdom start raining out.

And as if by the hand of God
A grassy carpet forms on the sand so hot
The raindrops of wisdom are spreading love
A wonderful kindness coming from high above

On the grass, soulful flowers start to grow
And all over, gentleness and harmony flow
In the meantime, still wisdom is pouring out
From that wonderful apple cloud.

Oh, no my friends, this is not just a dream,
In our world now still full of greed, soon will stream:
A flow of love causing a true wisdom revolution:
That will be the pinnacle of God's planned evolution!

<u>Come and touch my heart</u>

Come and touch my heart;
it is made of soft satin,
of delicate silk.

Come and touch my heart
with a finger of sadness,
with a tearful eye
and I will be sad with you.

Come and touch my heart
with a finger of joy,
with smiling face
and I will be joyful with you.

Come and touch my heart;
it's made of softness;
it is filled with love;
it wants to feel with you.

Fragrance

Making someone else feel good about themselves is
like planting a flower along the path of your life.

Making someone else feel small or stupid is
like throwing some toxic waste on your life's path.

If we look back at our yesterday's path
does it carry the wonderful fragrance of flowers or
does it smell more like toxic waste.

It does not matter too much. What really matters, is
to ensure that today is filled with the amazing fragrance of
making people feel good. 😎

Enjoy the path.

Watering Plants

There are a few rules for watering plants effectively, like the best time is early in the morning; it is better to give fewer times a lot of water than more frequently small amounts; and a few other tips that are easily available on the web.

I am not writing this to provide tips for watering plants, but I want to address the simple joy it brings. We cannot water plants without imagining how it will benefit them. And that is such a joy. Even if we do something good for plants, the joy is ours as much as the benefits that go to the plants.

And that is so if we treat animals right as well. Feeding a stray cat, taking care of a pet. So much happiness hidden in these simple acts.

But the biggest joy and peace of mind still comes, when we do something nice for our fellow human beings. Random kind acts are so valuable to our peace of mind and happiness that it is difficult to live without them. Whether we are on the receiving or giving end, it always brings joy to both the giver and the receiver of kindness. Let us be fully aware this giant truth for the coming hour, the coming day, the coming week,...

Hey, Hey People of Every Nation

Hey, hey people of every nation,
please read this small but real calculation
If you do two random kind acts every day
That would be more than 700 in a year, Okay?

Hey, hey women and men of every nation
please read this small but real calculation
Now nobody, really nobody is immune to kind acts
but assume only ten percent would have some effects

Hey, hey poets and readers of every nation
please read this small but real calculation
That would mean every year 70 persons would be inspired
by 1 person living a life of kindness without getting tired

Hey, hey poets and readers of every nation
please read this small but real calculation.
That means that just 1/70 or less than 1.5 percent
needs to believe, to touch the whole world by year end

Hey, hey people of every nation
please read this small but real calculation
Let's hurry to be part of this 1.5% choosing to be kind
Please people listen to your soul, your heart and mind

Hey, hey women and men of every nation
please read this small but real calculation
Join quickly the revolution of kindness and bliss
You will never regret, reading and reacting on this

Hey, hey readers of every nation
please read this small but real calculation

Breathe

We like to breathe clean air
We need to breathe for our bodies to survive
If we stop breathing, we die in a very short time
If we end up in a town with lots of haze and pollution,
Do we stop breathing?
Even if our air is polluted, we will continue to breathe
Because breath is essential to survival of our body

We like to love lovely people
We need love for our happiness to survive
If we stop loving, our happiness dies in short time
If we end up among unloving greedy people
Do we stop loving?
It is wise, even in a toxic environment to keep loving
Because to love is essential for the survival of our happiness

On a Parking...

A lovely flower spouted from a tiny seed
it'd worked its way through a split in the concrete
but it managed to grow and finally succeed
'cause beauty was not a mere desire but a need

Tuning In

If we try to tune in, into that ever present creative force and source of wisdom in the universe, many of us call God, we may find that he created us in a very special way. We find pleasure (short lasting) in food and other physical or material gains (like most animals do) but we can find bliss, happiness and lasting peace of mind through selfless altruism and random kind acts. More and more people are discovering this giant truth and whether or not they believe in God, they still get the enormous bliss from their humanitarian efforts. The wisest among us are the biggest humanitarians, whether we believe in God or not. Just as we do not have to know Steve Jobs to use the I-phone, we do not have to know God to make full use of our God-given heart and soul qualities. For anyone searching for true happiness, altruism is a NEED

Get Ready

Get ready
Get ready for beauty
Get ready, Man
Get ready, M'am
Get ready boys and girls

Beauty is in the sky
Beauty on the water, under the water
On the ground, in the ground, under it
In your soul, in your heart, in your mind
It is in the eyes, on the face
Beauty is everywhere
Get ready for a beautiful day

Get ready
Get ready for wisdom
Get ready, Man
Get ready, M'am
Get ready, boys and girls

Wisdom is in the sky
It is everywhere on the rise
It lies in the random kind act
In the books, in your smile
On the net, in the work we do
In the prayers we say.
Wisdom is on the rise

Get ready,
Get ready for kindness and love
Get ready, Man
Get ready, M'am
Get ready boys and girls

Kindness is coming
It is in a bullet train, an unstoppable TGV
Millions on board already
Gathering momentum, Exponential increases
The train moves at dazzling speed
With open doors, sucking in more and more people
Soon a billion will be on board
Then it will take only seconds
To envelop the whole wide world.

Get ready for a beauty revolt
Get ready for a wisdom revolution
Get ready for a huge kindness revolution.

Time

What do we use the bulk of our time for? A simple question that propped up in my mind.

While I have a deep conviction that pure peace and happiness lies more in altruism than in anything else, I have to admit that only fragments of my time are truly spent in selfless service.

Life is time and time is limited.

While we need to spend time for self development, self renewal at all aspects of life (physical, intellectual, emotional, spiritual,...), i decided to search in mind actively how i can optimize the use of my time.

I want to spend a bit more time in altruism, not the self aggrandizing type of philanthropy, but in simple kindness, in going the extra mile, in simple selfless service.

Opportunities to Be Kind

At the start of the day,
yes, every morning I pray
to become aware and see
any simple opportunity
to perform a random kind act.

Sometimes it is a simple thing
like a giving way to a man waiting
or a simple nice word to someone in need
a simple smile to a stranger I meet
but it always has a miraculous effect.

Last week I was in a hurry on my way to work
but we never know where opportunity 'll lurk
I saw a skinny man dressed in absolute rags
looking for something of value in the trash
He hoped that he could find something worthwhile

I was quite late, and it was almost nine
I thought I will help the man next time
But then I thought and changed my mind
A U-turn to act on the opportunity to be kind.
I gave him something that gave him a bright smile.

I think he was happy and certainly I was too
A simple kind act is always worth to do

Nature's Whisper

A soft whisper from nature has entered my breath
I swallowed and inhaled it to my lungs' deepest depth
and now it is tickling my heart and my mind
It keeps humming a song of love and being kind

Whenever I feel lazy to give help to a friend,
it will make me reach out anyhow a loving hand.
The small voice gives me peace and harmony;
it awakens a sense of the beauty of reality

It encourages me to stop living based on my greed
It reminds me that grace and love is a much bigger need.
Dear small whisper of nature, please do not leave me
I cherish you so much, feel welcome to stay eternally

Empathy

If we practice empathy regularly, we are accessing one of the biggest gifts of our Universe to humans. It is such a great tool to understand our world, our fellow human beings better, to become more patient and more kind, more loving, more forgiving. It is such a great tool to obtain more peace of mind not only for ourselves but also to help attain this to others. It is such a great tool to live a happier and more fulfilling life.

Empathy requires imagination and the more we practice our own imagination, the stronger it becomes. I encourage everyone to practice every day imagining something very nice happening in this world, that would change it forever. It will boost your own sense of gratitude and peace and who knows, if enough people imagine daily something very nice to happen to the world, it may become a reality sooner rather than later :)

The Wisdom Tortoise

While taking a walk, I heard a squeak
I looked and there right at my feet
Was a tortoise who seemed very slow
Why it squeaked, I didn't know

I looked it into the eyes for awhile
And tried to please it with a smile
The tortoise looked up and said with a wail
'Just now, my friend, you stepped on my tail'

"Oh, did I? " My voice was filled with regret
I should better look where my feet, I set
I expressed how I felt sorry,
And asked it to please forgive me

'Of course, I will forgive you
Even if not asked for, I always do
Forgiveness is an integral part of me, you see
I am the wisdom tortoise, that's what they call me'

"Wow", said I, "so you must love philosophy"
'Oh no', she cried, 'that is not for me'
"But love of wisdom is what means philosophy"
'If that's so, it has disintegrated terribly'

'The wisdom that I love and adhere to
May be far too simple for you
It is all about loving and being kind
Since that is what brings us peace of mind'

‘I do not bother about the reasons for being
Neither about the ghosts some of us are seeing
It is all so simple for me
Unconditional kindness is the way to be’

"Oh wisdom tortoise, what a pleasure to meet you here
Wisdom and kindness is also to me extremely dear
I believe that the next step in the evolution
Is a wisdom and kindness revolution"

The tortoise nodded and agreed with this
Kindness simply means happiness and bliss.
I thanked the tortoise and there our ways did part
To meet her again is still a wish sitting in my heart.

And the Winner Is...

Mike A and John K had a quarrel.
Mike was very upset with John.
He scolded John and called him an extremely nasty name.
Having been friends for a long time, the name calling was
hurting John badly.
In John's head there was pool of nasty names appearing
that would equal of even exceed the one he received just now.

In the time it took find the most nasty name,
the soul of John nudged him.
He remembered a saying, he had read somewhere,
'first try to understand before being understood'

Even though John felt he was not at fault for the subject of
the quarrel,
he tried to understand the anger of Mike.
He left in his mind,
the pool of nasty names behind and within seconds,
his heart made him reply:
"It must be hard on you, Mike, I understand"

This totally unexpected answer took Mike off guard.
His perturbed mind became a bit more peaceful
He was aware of the mean name he had called his friend and
the kind answer he received.

He suddenly tried to understand why Mike had done the thing that upset him so much.
A wave of remorse for the name calling entered his heart and he almost instantly apologized.

They managed to talk in a gentle way and agreed that there had been a misunderstanding.
John agreed not to do the things that were upsetting Mike so much again and Mike agreed
to try to look at it from a different point of view.

The friendship was blooming and it felt good for both.
And the winner was...

~ KINDNESS! ~
(it always is...)

The Spark

When our future seems just gloomy and dark
It is time to search for that amazing spark
That is always there, that never goes out
No matter how grey the sky, how dark the cloud.

No matter how disturbing the news, we read
We can always find what we truly need
Let's not seek it on Facebook, no, not on the net
That spark is not there, let's never forget

It sits inside, in our brain, our heart and soul
That spark of passion, that burning call
that little motivating flame to be ever nice and kind
that inspiring thought that never really left our mind

Let's go on a complete fast from news at least for a day
Let us make it silent within and keep all negativity at bay
Find back that spark inside and feed it
A flame, a fire of **passion for kindness**, we truly need it

Ambition

I was very ambitious by all means
My true desire was winning forever
The top of the rank was in all my dreams
Wanting to be the best, the most clever.

I got always in front; winning, I did
I outwitted and surpassed many others.
But inside, I felt not good about it
Whenever I had put down my brothers.

Along the way, many lessons, I've learned
There's no peace in being atop of all
It takes lots of care and being concerned
To find happiness in our heart and soul

Now, it is extremely clear in my mind.
My one ambition is: simply be kind

A Straight Road

True happiness is hidden in a thick curtain of smoke.
The media and all the adds we see want to make us believe
that happiness lies in things; in getting drunk; in smoking;
that happiness lies in controlling others; in getting power,
and as such, they create a lot of smoke on the highway to
happiness,
causing many of us getting stuck on the sideways, on the
premature exits.

The highway to happiness is kindness.
Simple kind acts, simple loving deeds alight the happiness
from within.
Living a life of love and beauty of kindness and creativity
lights up flames inside.
It lightens our mood; gives us peace of mind, peace of heart,
peace of soul

The highway to happiness: Let us stay on the highway,
no matter how much smoke unscrupulous industries blow
over the road
with deceiving advertisements

The highway to happiness:
A straight road filled with kindness

We Have to Experience It and Discover It Through Reflection on Experience!

It was 1988 and I was in the final year of Medical School in the University of Gent, Belgium. A patient had been brought to the hospital by ambulance. It was a homeless man who had been found on the sidewalk of a city street, in a pool of blood that he apparently had vomited out. He was drowsy and in the emergency department (ED) he had received a pint of blood, which had made him more alert. After his treatment in the ED, he was sent to the 3rd floor, where I was posted with 2 of my friends.

He was the archetype of a homeless man, with a long beard and long unkempt hair. He wore the patient's hospital attire, but one could imagine how his clothes must have looked like when he was found on the pavement. We had to take his medical history but that did not go very smoothly. Next, the physical examination was also not the easiest to perform. About an hour later we met him in the corridor, and he was asking if there were any playing cards available. He wanted to play Solitaire. There were certainly no decks of cards available there and the best advice we could come up with was to ask him to try the hospital's convenience store.

It had not been a busy day and by 5.00 pm I was on my way home, which was about 15 minutes from the hospital. Along the way, thoughts of the homeless man bothered me. Why did we not even try to properly help him to get some playing cards? We knew very well there were no playing cards for sale in the convenience store. Even if there were, the man would not have had the money to buy them.

When I arrived home, I went straight to our cupboard where we kept the playing cards. In Belgium in the late 1980s, almost every family had several decks of playing cards in the house. I took a new deck and drove back to the hospital. I rushed up to the floor where the man was admitted and gave him the cards. His smile was worth a fortune, and it touched my heart in a special way. I, too, was smiling when I drove home. The following day we found him in his room still playing Solitaire. Some of the cards were covered with saliva and the deck looked anything but new anymore, but the man was happy.

The above may be quite an insignificant event. Just a simple act of kindness. But it stands out clearly in my own memory, as an important turning point in my life. As a young man in his early 20s, I often tried to reflect about my own experiences as a medical student. The day I met the homeless man, I managed to reflect at night and think about life.

I wondered what it was that made me go back to the hospital, just to give this stranger a deck of playing cards. I thought even more about where that fantastic feeling came from when I saw the broad smile across his face. It was the truest and most authentic type of happiness that I had felt, while driving back home after handing the cards to the man.

Most of my friends and I had been searching for happiness through leading a full and social life by partying, socializing among friends, and by seeking material things, leisure and vacations. And right there in my heart, in my soul, had entered a feeling of peace, love and joy, that was bigger than any bodily pleasures I could imagine.

My thoughts turned to years before, when I had received a radio alarm clock as a Christmas present. At the time, it was a new invention that allowed me to wake up with music instead of with the loud sound of a regular alarm clock. I was very excited to receive such a fantastic gift. But the excitement soon waned. I soon became used to waking up to music, and quite often I would wake up to the voice of a disc jockey instead of music. At first the numbers silently moved each minute, but with time the movements grew louder and louder and it just became noise to me. I ended up wishing away the radio alarm clock.

While excitement comes in huge doses, especially for material gains and possessions, it tends to not last very long. The quality of the type of happiness and short-term excitement experienced upon achieving material gains, is very different from the quality of happiness and long-lasting positive emotions we feel when we genuinely and selflessly make another person happy. The peace of mind and feelings of love that come with it are so different.

While it seemed to me the discovery of a giant truth all by myself, it certainly was not so. I was blessed with an extremely loving and caring mother. I have learned a lot about love and care from her. Throughout my childhood, she tried to teach us empathy and compassion, and one of the effective ways was through making bread. ☺

The Bread Story

Have you ever kneaded bread by hand? It is a bit like a boxing ball, just softer and more fun! As a child, I loved it whenever my mother baked her own bread. I liked the process of making it more than eating it, though. After baking, my mother would ask me to ride my bicycle and bring one of the loafs to her 80-year-old aunt, who lived 8 kilometers from our house. Aunty had lived an exciting and challenging life but was now old and lived alone.

Once the bread popped out of the oven, I would hop on my bicycle to bring one to auntie. She would be sitting next to an old coal stove, and when I arrived, her small, curved body would rise from the chair and greet me with one of the most beautiful smiles. She was visibly happy. She would offer me lemonade and sweets and asked me lots of questions and laughed at my answers. She was always happy to meet me. I am not sure how much my mother had intended to teach through these 'bread rounds", but it certainly taught me how to be affable with the elderly. I cherish those moments when I entered the house bearing freshly baked bread, only to leave an old lady with a look of sheer happiness on her face.

Adding It Up

I was certainly blessed with a superb mother, and I think that many of us also claim to have the best mother in the world. Mothers want above anything for their children to be happy. We are taught to be nice and good, but quite often the influence of our "friends" and peers in schools or universities urges us to discover other "truths" as well. That is why it is important that we discover the good, real truths about kindness, or re-discover these truths through our own experiences and our own reflection to make such truths an integral part of our life.

Both experience **AND** reflection are necessary ingredients to discover good principles and values that will guide us on the path that our Creator intended for us. If we want our children to walk along a path filled with peace and caring and love, we need not only to plant some seeds, but also to teach them to *think and reflect about their own experiences* and notice their thoughts and feelings about them.

About Old Typewriters and Greed

There is a new vision of life:
It involves kindness without strife
It is the vision of sharing our time and all things
and enjoy the sheer happiness it brings.

There is no feeling-good in abuse and greed
No joy in the feeling of an ever-increasing need,
If we cannot change our old views of success
we may forever chase but never find happiness

Soon greed will survive only in a small minority
since more and more of us start seeing the superiority
of practicing kindness love and simply sharing
of living a life filled with compassion and caring

There are some old typists who still want to use
only old typewriters since computers, they refuse
There are still people clinging to greed and division
not willing to accept life's new kindness filled vision.

Obviously old typewriters are absolutely obsolete
Soon this will be true also for the stupidity of greed
We will all value that happiness and peace of mind
only originates from love, sharing and being kind.

Evening Reflection

This morning I wanted to be the sunshine
in the life of everyone I'd meet

Now at night, I am not so sure
Not sure if any rays have shone

Sometimes small gestures or a kind word
can make a difference in someone's life

I hope I had some of these today
'cause of big good deeds I am not aware

Perhaps the small talk with my son
or an unobtrusive hi or smile

I still hope that my day has meant a thing
for here or there a soul, a heart or mind

The Extra Step

Every now and then, we feel satisfied
So satisfied with what we feel and do
We have a good heart and are often kind
Occasionally some charity too.

But my God, my good Creator, today
I want to take at least one extra step
An extra mile along that golden way
Please God help me to run an added lap

If every day, a few new steps we take
One more small kindness and a loving phrase
An enormous difference we would make
Towards a better world in many ways

Let's commit each day to a little more
Soon harmony will reign on every shore

Abundance

Waves of enchanting orange morning light
broke on the shore of sand so white.
The sea, coloured by it in pastel, wonderfully,
whispered to the sun, a bit angrily:

'Hey, this is MY shore, to break my waves.
Please, dear sun, take back your wavy rays'.

The sun, smiling a warm, kind smile at once,
explained gently, the principle of abundance:
'Of everything created, God gives more than enough
We can truly share all things on earth with love'.

Yes! Good Morning

A big blue whale came to meet me
while I was swimming in the sea.
Hi mister whale, how are you today?
What's up, what brought you this way?

Whale: " my friend, you may believe it or not,
but I have a short message from our all-loving God:
A tonne of love sits inside your heart, you know,
please, Hans, let it flow, let it flow."

If we let it flow from within, all that love
we will receive so many blessings from above;
not only for ourselves, but truly to all people we know
imagine a world filled with love, yes just let it flow.

And then the whale returned to the deeper part of the sea
with a big splash that seemed to have awakened me.
What a wonderful dream, so close to the break of the day.
I love the message and plan certainly to follow that way. :)

The Miracle of Kindness Has Become Undestroyable

I feel the need to say a small prayer for this big world
The unique part of our human nature is our happiness
which depends on being good and helping other humans

We have evolved from warring tribes into many loving
communities
And that is one of the biggest miracles that have happened
in this world
But a few barbaric people have grabbed power through
endless lies

Please, our God, let this huge work and that superb miracle
of having truly loving, helping and free communities around
the world
not go to pieces, because of a few handfuls of power-sick
greedy minds,
for whom billions of dollars seem never enough.

The peace that was in the air this morning
The love that was surrounding my own community
The superb altruism that has evolved.

So precious. On the surface they seem fragile
But the roots reach deep and let the forest of kindness
be soon lush again, filled with blossoms of Love.

That amazing Love with capital L

Roots in Everyone's Heart

There is a tree
A wonderful tree.
The tree of kindness.
It is the fastest growing tree
In this world, God bless

There is a tree
The wonderful kindness tree
Taking deep roots forever to last
In a million people's heart
Spouting and growing enormously fast

There is a tree
That wonderful kindness tree
It grows so fast, that soon enough
The whole wide world on sea and earth
will be filled with comfort and love

There is a tree
That wonderful tree of kindness
Roots spreading in another million hearts
spouting and growing reaching high and wide
And then in another million hearts it starts

And then another two million
And five million more to come
A billion hearts soon will follow
I already smell its wonderful blossom
Roots in everyone's heart will show

Oh, it is growing so fast,
this tree let's sit and enjoy
in its amazing shadow
And just let the roots
in your heart grow!

The Balloon

I went to the sea of love, this noon
I took it and put it in a blue balloon

I brought this balloon so blue
all the way, especially for you

So, quick, quick, quick
Give this balloon a prick

Let's bathe in its content
A Sea of love, to never end

Colours of Love

Colours of love sit in the depth of our heart.
It is high time for the painting to start.
Let's splash these colours of love and peace
on the walls and streets for all to please.
The colours of kindness, warmth and bliss;
all souls 'll be touched by paintings like this.

The astonishing hues of wonderful attraction
will cause nothing less than a chain reaction.
You may choose to believe it or not:
in no place, the painting will stop.
Tints of love and kindness 'll glow everywhere
and no, the painting will not stop there.

It 'll go on 'til the whole land is covered in love:
kindness in front, from behind, below and above.
All my brothers and sisters 'll use their brush,
spreading colours so adorable, vibrant and lush
until all children in our whole world wide
will enjoy love's bliss and kindness' light.

Let us all take up our biggest brush today
and start painting the world, right away.

A Little Tree

One day, I found in a spot
Not so far from the sea
I thank you so much, my God
A lovely, wonderful tree

Its fruits, I started eating.
They were filled with love.
And I could not help but think
that I'd never get enough

One of the seeds of the fruit,
I have planted it in my soul
And now it's a pleasure to look
And watch a little tree grow.

~

And here comes a sonnet:

The Golden Key

One day, I want to melt all gold on earth
And make a wonderful key with it all
This special key of incredible worth
Will be fit to unlock your heart and soul

The remote buttons will work like a smile
Like a lawine of sweet and loving words
I will turn that key with a manly style
And happy thoughts will fly to you as birds

A simple turn of the sweet golden key
Just like a wonder, magic fun and true
Will cause, for everyone to hear and see
A wave of peace and happiness in you

Let's dream of a universe filled with love
And all may get a key from High Above

Fragile

I like to think about greed
as one of the most fragile things on earth:
as snow covering a field, facing the sun of an eternal spring,
as a porcelain vase standing in the middle of a football field,
as a piece of paper, once strong, but now getting awfully wet,
as a once strong leaf, now brown and rusty, ready to release
its branch
as a race car going too fast on a winding mountain road
as a house made of cards in the middle of a busy playground
as a nettle standing along the road side, soon to mowed

I like to think about wisdom
as the replacement of greed:
as the field blooming and blossoming in the sun of wisdom
as a strong football bouncing back whenever kicked
as a box of stainless steel overflowing with kindness
as a stem of a 300 year old tree ready to live another 500
as a bullet train getting filled with passengers lovely and kind
as a magnificent house where everyone is always welcome
as a field of evergreen grass surviving no matter how often it
is cut

The ice age of greed is about to leave us for the eternal spring
of wisdom
Kindness, peace, love, wisdom, caring, helping, inspiring, are
the new money :)

Nano

Some nano-molecules of joy
have entered my heart this morning
while I was cleaning a bit of my garden

Some nano-molecules of peace
have entered my mind this morning
when I saw and heard some beautiful birds

The nano-molecules of joy and peace
initiated a chain reaction of love
All love hidden inside, suddenly bared

Good Men

I always tell my son:

"We are good men. You and me are good men.
If someone does nasty things to us,
this does not change us from good to nasty.
We just choose to remain good men.
In case we would respond to nastiness
with our own nastiness,
then we would allow the nasty men
to turn us, who are good men,
into nasty men.
We are good and have chosen to be good
We do not give the power to anyone
to take away our goodness."

So if someone treats us good,
we treat them good.
If someone treats us in a nasty way,
we treat them good.
If someone ignores us
we treat them good

No one can take away our goodness :)

PS: of course we are not perfect, we do lose our temper sometimes,
we are not "always" good. But if we stray, we will choose not to do so for long.
We will try to quickly come back to be just...... good men

The Rose, Named Love

Overnight, in the garden I own,
a little red rose, named Love, had grown

Seeing its glory, I knew from the start
I had to pluck it, place it in my heart

From this exquisite rose, I am giving away
to my friends, a petal or two, every day

And of magical petals, I have no lack
'cause for each petal I give, two grow back

A big rose named Love will as long as I live
fill up my heart: tonnes of petals to give

Now quick, I am sure that in your garden too,
there will be a magic rose, named Love, for you

The Light of Love

A black angel and a white angel kiss;
rainbow colours adorn their wings.

The kiss becomes a halo of joy and bliss;
a tender light of love starts glowing

The light turns into a mighty star, a sun,
shining rays of love for every man and woman.

It all started with a lovely kiss
between two angels, black and white!

Human

No matter how good our intentions,
we are all human at any time.

I have written a lot about kindness and my belief in a kindness revolution.
Today, I had quite a stressful day and lost my temper not once but twice.

Luckily nobody saw both events but even those seeing one of the events,
may say, is that the strong writer and "preacher" of kindness?

I think these are real lesson in humility.
We believe in values and principles,
but being human, we cannot live up to them all the time.

Does this mean we should not write or talk about them?
I think we should not judge anybody when they are not kind or loving.
None of us is always kind and loving since we are simply humans.

However, if we are silent about our beliefs and values,
all the negativity in the world will go without any bit of balance.

So i choose not to feel too guilty about losing my temper on and off

even though I try so very hard not to get angry at any time.
Let us talk and write a lot about kindness and the values we believe in;
it may make us stronger in the practice of these principles and values.
At the same time let's be humble, do not judge others and accept our own limitations

Lots of wishes for love and peace to all of you (and for myself too 😌 😊 😌)

Far Away...

Somewhere far away,
in another galaxy,
there is a little star
that started to shine
several years ago.

Its light is traveling
at a dazzling speed
towards our planet
with a message of love
a message of kindness.

Less, much less now
than a light year away
that lovely little light
from that tiny star
will reach us soon.

Once it reaches,
no heart 'll remain shut;
all the beauty and love
will enter freely
into all humanity

Oh, little star
let your light come
and keep on shining
for a world, a planet
that needs you oh so much.

Kindness Nearer Than Ever

The world seems to become less and less friendly as a place to live in.

Please do not fall for this great fallacy!

There are no real statistics about friendliness and caring societies.
One thing, I am perfectly sure however, is that the picture we get
from the news is a WRONG picture.

True enough, what happens in the USA is troublesome.
What happens in so many other countries is troublesome

But we see only the troublesome things in the news.
Good news seems to be not "newsworthy" these days.

The idea of a worldwide caring society
The idea of eradication of hunger in the world
The idea of peace
The idea of a kindness revolution

These are all ideas (and there are many more) whose time has come.
Perhaps what we see in the US is a necessary evil to speed up the final

collapse of the opposites of the above ideas.
Like waves gaining momentum as they near the shore,
but collapsing on the shore,
the life of these ideas (like selfishness, fear mongering,...)
will totally, absolutely and irreversibly end.

While they collapse on the shore they may cause damage
but never will the mountain of justice
the mountain of kindness
the mountain of caringness
the mountain of love
the mountain of respect
be moved by any of these vicious waves.

Please, my friends,
Stop reading all that negativity,
keep building within your own society
on a principle of caring kindness.

The kindness revolution is my favorite idea whose time has
come
Its time is really here and nothing will stop it.

River Meets Desert

A young river,
So strong
Nothing could stop it
Nothing went wrong

Big rocks in its way
No problem at all
It went over them
Around them if tall

But then it met the desert
Water sank deep into sand
Huge problem for the river
It looked like its life was to end

Desperately
It turned to our God
'Please, God help me
To get away from or over this spot'

A voice from above said
'Look at the wind in the sky
It crosses the desert so easily
So just stop to cry! '

'But I am not wind, I am water
How can I cross
Please help me
I am at a loss'

'Did you forget dear river, '
Said the voice from above
'Long time before you were a river
The wind carried you with love'

The river let its water evaporate
Allowed the wind to carry it once more
In its loving arms,
wind held the river as before

Across the desert they went
A lot of water in a big large cloud
And at the other side
The wind let it rain out

There the river again became strong
Even better and stronger than before
With much vigour it ran
For everyone to adore

Dear young men and women alike
If you meet with the desert or anything wrong
Remember who carried you
Before you became a river so strong

Should Be Like This

This afternoon having with my lovely wife, a coffee and a piece of cake in the coffee shop. Shortly after we sit down, the woman at the table next to us announces that the battery of her phone was almost flat. She was sitting alone at the table and clearly was telling this to my wife. She plugged the telephone into a power bank. She asked my wife whether she was from Kuantan and a nice conversation followed.

As we were sitting there her daughter and her nephew came and sit with her and she asked the two children to shake hands with us.

I thought the encounter was a bit unusual. People in a coffee shop or even on a bus tend to be too shy or too afraid of rejection to start a conversation. Really each time I started a conversation on a plane with the person next to me, I have enjoyed it. I always make plans to do it more, but all too often we are not doing it.

Easy communication, friendliness, kindness, can make all our world so much nicer.

Quarks Inside

The morning sunlight
In all its glory
The morning sunlight
In all its glam

Every molecule in my heart
Is jumping up and down
The quarks inside collide
Emanating a mini beam of light

I hope that this little beam of light
Coming from my heart in a way
Can just like the morning sun
Brighten the lives of those I meet today

True Nature

This is a small prayer
for all people
in this big world
to become aware
of our true nature
which is love
which is kindness
which is compassion
which is peace
which is harmony.

A small prayer
for all of us
to become aware
that only a life
filled with our true nature
is THE source of
true happiness

Help me, my God,
Help all my friends
all my family
all my colleagues
all my neighbours
and all, all others
in this big world
to love, be kind, compassionate
and be an instrument of
Your peace and harmony

The Mountain Gone

My soul has no hands and no feet
but it ran over the mountain
that stood between you and me
It dug a hole in the soil
and planted a fine young tree

The roots soaked up all earth
that had made up the mountain

Soon the mountain was gone
and a majestic tree
provided some shadow
to love forever, you and me
in perfect harmony

Electric!

Electricity existed at the time Moses was walking the earth.
Electricity existed at the time Julius Caesar was walking the earth
Electricity existed at the time Napoleon was walking the earth

Was it God's fault they were walking in the dark
Was it God's fault they had no light?

Surely not. It is just that humanity needed to evolve
to a level that someone could discover the light bulb
to discover electricity, to discover batteries...

Now we use electricity to perhaps its best level.
We enjoy it

Kindness existed in olden times
Kindness existed in the nineteenth century
Kindness exists in the 21st century.

Peace and unconditional love and universal kindness
are now here already in this world.
They have always been.

But somehow many of us are still walking in the dark
in the darkness of greed and strive and racism and nationalism
But the good news is that the time is ripe.

It is in these exciting times that we are evolving perhaps enough
to kindness materialize and fully be expressed for all human beings.

Peace is here.
Unconditional love is here
Universal kindness is here
Let us just open up.
The time is ripe
Let these three come to universal expression.

A spoon full of life
with a pinch of love on it:
Truly Delicious

Amazing Flowers of Love

If your words contain seeds of hatred
I will catch them before they enter my heart
I will remove them from my being
Crush them, destroy them, flush them away

If your words contain seeds of love
I will open all doors and let them in
I will plant them in the soil of my heart
And let them bloom into amazing flowers

Amazing flowers of love

Let us not allow politicians, religious bigots or anyone else
to manipulate us into any form of hatred.

Let us choose love.
Let us guard the doors of our mind and heart
and NOT let in any words that cause us to hate
Let us open the doors of our mind and heart
for any words that encourage to love :)

<u>I love, thus I am - J'aime, donc je suis.</u>
It was Descartes who said: Je pense, donc je suis, I think, thus
I am.
I want to suggest a small change to my 'friend' Descartes:
I love, thus I am: J'aime, donc je suis.

First, a small poem:

I Love, Thus I Am

I am,
I love.
A white rolling wave
in the blue ocean
whispers in my ear:
You are,
You love.
I want to thank the wave,
I want to love the wave,
but before I can,
it breaks on the shore
and ceases to be.
I am,
I love.
The beauty of the wave,
Its silent whisper
are still so much alive.
When I close my eyes
I see and hear it:
You are,
You love!

And not only we, as a being, are! The love we created, the kindness poured out of our hearts,
comes into existence from nothing. Not only it exists in the moment, but it goes on living
many years after our kind act. Perhaps for eternity.

The small wave in the poem, was so kind and whispered such a sweet words to me,
that the wave goes on living in my memory and its kind words are as much alive
now as when the wave was whispering them.

Of course the poem is a metaphor.
I hope it is powerful enough for everyone to embrace the truth in:
J'aime, donc je suis
or perhaps better still: J'aime, donc je serai
I love, thus I am
or perhaps better still: I love, thus I will be (forever). :)

Harmony

Harmony has been on my mind this morning.
Actually it is on my mind quite often.
Really, I think that harmony in this world is possible
Many people may doubt it is to happen very soon but
On mornings like today, I get really convinced that
Nothing can stand in the way of the ever increasing harmony.
Yes, harmony is a thought whose time has come

We will soon see that love will reign
In our house, in our village in our state
Love will reign in the whole wide world
Love will win over greed and crime and fights

Soon we will see harmony in our world, everywhere, all the time.
On every corner of the street we will see smiles and lovely faces
On every field, in every house we will meet friendliness and
kindness
Nastiness and quarrels and ill will will be a thing of the past

Believe that this may happen. The more people believe, the
sooner it will happen
Every person on earth has the right to harmony and we can
make it happen.

Harmony is in my dream, harmony is in my mind, in my heart.
Every soul on earth has this silent longing to live a
harmonious life
Right now is the time, today is the time, let us no longer wait
Everyone can make a small contribution today toward lots of
harmony in the world

Touched

Touched by the tremendous love in the hall.
So many parents brought their disabled children to the health camp.
The very special bond and supreme love of these parents was so touching.
That love was filling the hall where the health camp was held.

Touched by the tremendous love in the hall.
More than 250 volunteers had worked so hard for days.
Their love and care for the disabled children, so heart warming.
The hall was truly filled with love.

I just came back from a health camp for disabled children (Johor).
There is sooooo much love in this world of 2017.
There is sooooo much love.

Much more love than hatred!
Much more love than sadness!
Much more love than wickedness!
Much more love than greed!

I do not worry for the future of the world.

While greed is still running high in some areas,
I am so sure love will be its master
While the world has still a lot of haters
Love will be their master

Yes, I was touched today, in so many ways
by the tonnes of love that were present in the hall of the health camp

The mass media (try to) portray that all bad things are on
the increase
and that love is shrinking fast in this world.
You and I, if we look at the people we know, at the world
around us,
we know better. Love is ever increasing, and wickedness and
hatred
are dying a slow but certain death.

Yes, I was touched today, in so many ways
by the tonnes of love that were present in the hall of the health
camp

It's an Ocean

Imagine a sea,
a large sea;
no, imagine an ocean,
A huge ocean
filled with love.

Within that ocean
we swim and
Enjoy its greatest depths
but so often we are not aware
we live in an ocean of love.

For family and strangers,
for friends and enemies,
just take a cup or two
and share a drink of love.

A bit of love, a few drops
is often all we need
to turn a dark moment
into a shining present.

A bit of love, a small cup
is often all we need
to turn a bout of stress
into an oasis of peace.

A bit of love, a sip or cup
is often all we need
to live a life of purpose,
to change the world.

The Sun and the Cave

This morning, I read the following powerful story and I do not want to wait another minute to share it with you all:
One day, the sun and a cave were talking to each other. The sun did not understand "dark and damp" and the cave did not understand what it meant by "bright and clear". So they decided to change places for awhile. First the cave went up to the sun and exclaimed: "Oh, how wonderful this all is!". Then they went to the place of the cave and as the sun entered, it said "I cannot see any difference!"

I think this story is 'soooo' powerful!
If you are the one emitting the light and warmth,
      it is quite impossible to experience the dark and cold.
If you are the one emitting peace of mind and serenity
      it is quite impossible to be disturbed and stressed
If you are the one bringing happiness to others
      it is quite impossible to be sad for a long time.
If you are the one bringing inspiration and encouragement
      you may never end up in the drab and gloom.

CREATIVITY

Accepting Imperfection

Somehow, the gifts of peace, beauty and love, magnificent as they are, tend not to be ours all the time.

While we all have experienced the exhilaration of observing an amazing piece of nature; while we have all experienced the heart melting moments of extreme love and courage, be it in stories, movies or real life; while all of us have been touched by moments of peace and silence; our lives are still all too often filled with stress and frustration about serious imperfections, serious problems, about ugliness, evil, and chaotic situations, about pain and disharmony.

One of the popular sayings by some scientists, defending their atheistic beliefs, goes as follows: If there would be a good God, he would be not almighty, if there would be an almighty God, he would not be good. These scientists are caught in their own box and time after time, I feel a bit disappointed by the weak response of the believers, of the people with faith.

It only would take a moment or two, for everybody to imagine the opposite of an imperfect world. Let us go on this imaginary trip. We wake up in a perfect world. No illness, no war, no theft, no anger, no pollution, just love, sweetness, pure perfection.

I would wake up perfectly rested after the most wonderful night of sleep. I would have a super delicious breakfast with all the nicest food, one can imagine. Then I would make a walk on a perfectly clean beach along the most beautiful deep azure, turquoise sea. I come home to take my shower and get in my dream-sports-car to drive off to work.

Here I would encounter a bit of a problem. My job that gives me so much satisfaction is that of a medical doctor. In a perfect world, no need for doctors, no need for engineers, no need for builders, no need for any job. Ok, I accept this, and would go for one of my hobbies, which is gardening. Another problem: whatever I would change to my perfect garden would make it worse. I may want to go and read a good book a write a poem, but in a perfect world, all knowledge would be mine already and all works of art would be available at our fingertips.

Anything we would do or any change we make would only make the world worse because it is perfect already.

What would happen to our motivation?
What would happen to our creativity?
What would happen to our drive?
What would happen to our good intentions?
What would happen to our job satisfaction?
What would happen to our peace of mind?

We humans thrive on creativity, on altruism, on making positive changes. Aren't these things essential components of success and peace of mind? Making a positive difference in our world seems an essential component of our true happiness. Would a perfect world not be endlessly boring? All doctors and nurses suddenly completely useless! Contractors, builders, courts, judges, politicians... no need

It looks like we were made not to live in a perfect world. Rather than an animalistic indulgence in good things, it appears that the good almighty God has intended to share the pleasure of **endless creativity** with us.:

* Suffering is here and we can do something to relieve it. Wow!
* People need help and we can help. Wow!
* Pain is inflicted and we can use our creativity and knowledge to alleviate it. Wow!
* Hunger and thirst. We were given food and drinks and are capable of sharing it. Wow!
* Sorrow and sadness exists, but we can console. Wow!
* Loneliness exists but we can love. Wow!

Sooner or later, all of us slowly come to be aware that true pleasure and happiness lies in relieving suffering, helping, in alleviating pain, in sharing, in consoling and loving. We will appreciate these greatest gifts of a loving and almighty Creator of our universe.

In our current reality there are people who need help.
In our current reality there are people who are helping.
We may move from needing help to helping and back and forth.

Surely it is better to be in the helping group but with an open mind we will be grateful for help rendered to us when we truly need it.

Just think for a while. Would we really want a perfect world? Or is the world, as it is, not too bad?

Our human brain is most likely far too small to fully understand all what happens in our world. I believe all what happens, happens for a reason. But not anyone can claim to understand why tsunamis, wars, earthquakes... are happening. Why diseases and premature death are happening.

A small poem here, explaining our lack of comprehension of what is happening in our world:

The Story of Why

There was once a one-year old boy
He was playing with a knife as a toy
He was having a real great time
How nicely did his lovely knife shine

Then came the father, got the surprise of his life.
As fast as he could, he took away the dangerous knife
The boy felt treated unfair and started to cry
His pleasure ended abruptly, he didn't know why

His tiny mind was not developed enough
to understand that it was his father's love
that was the reason why the knife was taken away
No way he'd understand what happened that day

It is also impossible for any of us to understand
the why of a tsunami or sudden death of a friend
we can go as deep as we can, we can try
but we never will reach the true answer to why.

Just our human mind's capacity is far too small
for us to understand the ultimate reason of all
I believe a supreme reason exists for everything
Sometimes we just have to accept what is happening...

Aufie Zophy

But I do understand that living in a perfect world, would be much worse than our current world. If there was no cold, who would appreciate warmth, if there was no death, would we really enjoy to live forever?

Let us celebrate the gift of creativity. Accept the many imperfections and make a positive difference!

A Very Special Prayer

I want to share here that wonderful prayer of St Francis from Assisi:

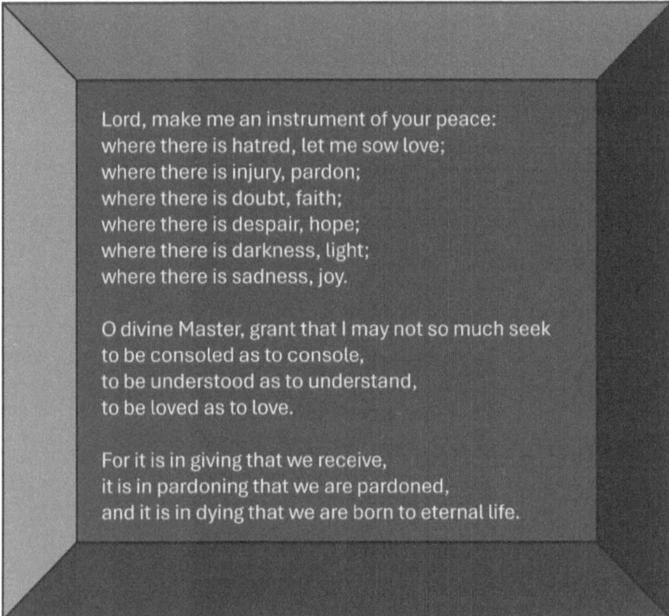

This simple prayer helps us to appreciate the creativity that lies in to love, to understand and to console, and the huge joy that is encompassed in these.
Here a personal story of this small prayer helped myself:
For many years I have chased being loved.
The more I chased it, the faster it ran away from me.

I work in Malaysia and when I came back to Europe, I expected from my closest family a very warm welcome. Small things that were not done or things that were done not to my liking, used to make me really unhappy and resulted in negative feelings that soon were translated in negative actions with more negativity coming my way.

Things changed when I read the prayer of Francis of Assisi. He was asking in that prayer to be given the strength so that he would hunger more **to love than to be loved** and **to understand rather than to be understood**. And that was really a game-changer for me. My next visit home in Europe, I decided to appreciate greatly whatever nice things were done to me (and believe me, if your focus is on that, you detect more than ever before) and to accept with an open and understanding heart whatever expectations that were not fulfilled. I had decided to love and not get lost in endless focusing on being loved.

Guess what, my next trip was one of the best ones ever. The love I received was so fantastic, so wonderful. I truly understood that paradox, it is in giving that we receive.

If enough people will commit
To make daily a small change
For anyone in their world,...
The world will be very different,
tomorrow already

How Clever!

How superbly clever must our Creator have been,
to create world with so many different people, so many
cultures, so many religions,
so many opinions, so many talents, so many perceptions, so
many convictions,
so many faiths, so many people who are each so extremely
unique!

How could anyone of us experience any growth,
any spiritual growth, emotional growth,
personality growth, character growth,
if we would all be the same, think the same,
feel the same, believe the same!

How superbly clever must our Creator have been!
How exciting is the eternal search of humans for the Truth
with capital T?
How superb is the feeling of discovering ancient texts that
said some things you felt for a long time already?

Let us today celebrate our many differences,
see the world as our biggest possible school
We can learn from/respect all our brothers and sisters.
Enjoy the differences between you and your family members,
the differences between you and your neighbours and friends,
the differences between you and your colleagues
the differences between you and all other people.

How unwise still are so many people
who lock themselves up in one single creed,
condemning to hell all people who think differently;
who refuse to even access the huge wealth of wisdom
found in nature, found in our own soul, found in the whole world.
If our faith is strong enough no need to be afraid of pluralism.
Pluralism is richness that can enhance your faith, ensure your continued growth.

Listening to others, reading widely, will help us understand, respect.
Of course we do not absorb all ideas offered in all we read or from whomever we meet.
We think, we critically analyse, keep our own faith, but increase our understanding and respect.

Let us today all benefit from our Creator's cleverness and open up to the whole world!

Truly Caring

You will enjoy this story, it's easy to understand.
It is about Wan Kamil, a wonderful friend.
In his garden, a small budding tree had grown
It was not planted; it seemed to have come on its own.

Wan Kamil figured out without too many words,
That it must have been animals, most likely birds,
That brought to his garden the seeds of this tree,
which has grown with many fruits, a pleasure to see.

The papayas on the tree are delicious and plentiful
and my friend Kamil, with a soul so beautiful,
understands perfectly nature's and animal's needs:
it are the birds that will spread more amazing seeds.

He leaves some of the papayas that are ripe on the tree
The animals and birds seem to have a feast for free
but in the process, they will ensure that in some place,
another papaya tree will grow by our Creator's grace.

Changing the World!

It is almost time to close my eyes, but before going to sleep, I want to make it a bit quiet within. I remember the song about love: ♪ *Let us love, love, love! Everybody, love, even when it is hard to love, our loving will change the world. Our sharing will change the world.*

Seems like some inner ramblings of my soul,
but it was something from you-tube,
I heard it perhaps more than a year ago,
but my memory had stored it in a safe place
for this giant truth to come back to me tonight:

Love, love, love
even if it is hard to love,
our loving will change the world
Share, share, share
even if it is hard to share,
our sharing will change the world

Let us all make it quiet for awhile
and let our soul sing these wonderful verses.
We will change the world!

Kindness and Peace!

We have evolved from warring tribes into many loving communities
And that is one of the biggest miracles that have happened
in this world
But a few barbaric people have grabbed power through endless lies

Please, our God, let this huge work and that superb miracle
of having truly loving, helping and free communities
around the world
not go to pieces, because of a few handfuls of power-sick greedy minds

The peace that was in the air this morning
The love that was surrounding my own community
The superb altruism that has evolved.

So precious. On the surface they seem fragile
But the roots reach deep and let the forest of kindness
be soon lush again, filled with blossoms of Love.

That amazing Love with capital L

The Path

There is a request in prayers every day
to be shown our God's path, His magnificent way
A simple request, Thy will be done on earth
A simple request; but what is it really worth
if it is not accompanied by any thorough reflection
if it is not followed by any meaningful action?

If we just ramble on, saying the words as fast as we can
how will our prayer benefit us or any other man?
Let us think during our prayer about what to do or not
to be on that path, to follow the will of our God.
Since the gifts and talents differ for me and for you
we really have to think for ourselves what we should do

In my imagination I see a diamond path, smooth and bright.
Being right in the middle brings us peace of mind, pure delight,
even if we just manage to be in the middle for a while.
It happens mostly just after we walk the figurative extra mile

When we went out of our way
to make a bit better the day
of a brother or sister, foe or friend,
in the middle of that path, we land.

A simple bout of anger or unfriendliness
and we sway off the path into a bout of stress
It puts us in the mud far from that way, into a mess
until our heart returns to love and kindness

I hope, my God, more often I can tune into virtue
because that brings us a bit closer to You
It brings us to that middle of that wonderful way
Let us be there, now, tomorrow and every day.

The Little Key

A small prayer
for kindness
for love

A soft longing
for affability
for friendship

A discrete desire
for compassion
for empathy

A simple want
for tenderness
for care

A minute search
for a smile
for a wink

Soul was praying,
longing, wanting
searching

A little softness
A little silence
A small key

A small key
to open the heart
A bit of silence

A gush of love
of kindness, of friendship
of big compassion

A huge stream
never ending
an open heart

An ocean of bliss
flooding the world
engulfing my soul

Silently gushing
quietly flooding
softly engulfing

A little prayer
A little longing
A little search

The key is never far away.

Creating Beauty

While the world is so full of beautiful natural scenes, our Creator has shared with us the gift of creativity and we can use our talents, our skills, our gifts to create pieces of beauty in the form of art.

All of us have the need to express ourselves: to share with the world what nature has communicated to us. We may have a talent for painting, for sculpting, for poetry, for any form of art.

The Most Beautiful Poem (Sonnet)

How I wish I would have the special words
To write the very most fantastic verse
I would pen it down with feathers of birds
write the nicest poem in the universe

I would dip the colourful plume in ink
That is magic and wonderfully blue
Using gothic letters of which I think
Anyone could see they were made for you

And this world would be full with jealous eyes
They would all be envying you so much
All people 'd turn their heads towards the skies
Wish a poem was written for them as such

But this one was for you and you alone
A superb poem, with a wonderful tone

Aufie Zophy

The Canvas

I want the new canvas of the day to look good
and thus I start with a loving, grateful mood:
with strokes of colour, soft and sweet pastel
I long to make a superb and pleasing aquarelle.

The heart, a good intention, adds a few red flowers
But oh what happens after only two or three hours?
The greed of my ego causing here and there some torment
Splashing on the painting hideous grey color of cement

I hope and pray that when I look tonight
I 'll have made the artwork look perfectly right
Perhaps looking like the most amazing flowery forest
Filled with acts of kindness, love and zest

Oh my Creator, full of grace, to you I pray
Guide me to make a masterpiece on the canvas of today.
Free of all harshness and splashes of hard concrete
Just pleasure, beauty, harmony, for the eye to meet.

Oh Poet, Oh Poem, Oh Poetry,

It is you who will change the world
From a wall infested street
To a magnificent orchard
To an adorable lavender field

Is it not you helping the world?
To see the magic in a drop of dew
Words rolling like breaking waves
To see the wonder in the monsoon
To see the miracles in normal days

It is you moving, softening hearts
To forgive, to create peace
To fill this world with loving minds
To dream the heavenliest dream
To make us kind and kind and kind

Is it not you, dear poetry,
Who will unchain us from avarice
And destroy disabling greed
Who will spray a soft and gentle mist
Of all-encompassing unconditional love

Poetry, hope for the future
Mover of souls
Mover of minds
Mover of hearts
Hope for the world

Passion and Poetry

A daily dose of passion and poetry
An inkling of inspiration
A resounding rhyme
A magnificent metaphor
A marvellous message
A soulful softness
An expression of ecstasy
An exquisite emotion

There is no more excellent elixir
No more perfect pills
than all the above
for the healing of our heart,
for the betterment of our body
for the solace of our soul
Where is my daily dose
Of passion and poetry?

FINAL CONSIDERATION

Are we really specs of dust in this giant universe?
Are we merely grains of sand on the shore of an endless sea?

I hope you have enjoyed this little journey, I hope it has
brought a little happiness.

A Speck of Significance

In the universe, a human so small,
Looking just like a speck of dust
But born with a mind and a soul
And able to think, love and trust.
Many think that as a human, just one
Not a positive change can be made, nothing great
What could a good deed selflessly done
Ever mean in a world full of hate?

But if a butterfly in India, flapping its wings
could cause a storm over the Atlantic
Just see how one of the small insignificant things
Can have an effect, so gigantic
Then why would your simple random kind act
Just by chance or by divine intervention
Not snowball and have a huge impact,
Perhaps a kindness revolt of enormous dimension

So in each of our lives we must
Make a choice of incredible importance
Do we want to be just a speck of dust
Or a speck of significance.

Aufie Zophy

And is there a better way to end this book than with a wonderful quote of Rumi?
"You are not a drop in the ocean. You are the entire ocean, in a drop".

All our experiences, all our thoughts, all our feelings, are a world, an ocean. All the beauty we have seen, all the love we have felt, all the care we have given or received, an ocean. And yet all too often we feel small and insignificant, while we are an ocean in a drop :)

Endless Sea

Am I merely a tiny grain of sand
on the shore of a sea without end?

But then, within that simple grain,
there sits a most amazing brain;
a heart filled to the brim with love;
a soul easily connecting to what is above.

Within this grain I find a giant peace;
a stream of love that 'll never cease;
an eye for beauty and harmony;
a soul full of passion for creativity.

Are we just a grain of sand or are we more?
We may well be a sea with sand on its shore?

Epilogue

Awareness of all gifts, the universe is giving us on a daily basis, appreciating the miracles of life, longing more to be than to have, longing more to love and understand than to be loved and to be understood,…. will elevate our life to a plane so far above the average.

We were meant to be here
We contribute to the evolution.
We accept the imperfections of our time
We contribute in our own special ways, no matter how small or big, to a world filled with kindness and love.

Keep the small diamonds of love, beauty and wisdom in this book. Keep them in your heart, keep them in your soul.

I wish you *awareness and all the happiness that flows from it.*

www.ingramcontent.com/pod-product-compliance
Lightning Source LLC
Chambersburg PA
CBHW051229130726
47988CB00001B/283